W9-DIR-727

GLOBETROTTER
TRAVEL GUIDE

Singapore

AFFLES HOTEL

HELEN OON

NEW
HOLLAND

1
Introducing Singapore

It was Sir Stamford Raffles' dream to transform this swamp-covered, pirate-infested island into a 'new Alexandria of the Far East'. His hopes for his new settlement were not misplaced: Singapore has since grown into an internationally important centre for trade, communications and tourism. It bears all the hallmarks of a great holiday destination: matchless tourist facilities, an excellent transportation system, superb hotels with all the sophistication and comfort of the West, and an enthralling melée of cultures.

It is a country of many contrasts. Hi-tech skyscrapers soar up among picturesque old buildings, and the people are still steeped in their ancient traditions, despite living in one of the most advanced countries in the world. You can step back in time amongst the beautiful buildings of the colonial district, but it is in the ethnic quarters of Chinatown, Arab Street and Little India that you will find the heart and soul of the city. Nature lovers will be surprised by the many pockets of green in this bustling city.

For the epicure, Singapore is one big scrumptious feast. There is some serious eating to be done in this United Nations of food, with styles ranging from Chinese, Malay and Indian to almost any international cuisine you might wish to try.

Singapore is a place to be included on any traveller's itinerary, whether for pleasure or business. Its manifold attractions lure over six million visitors to the Lion City every year.

TOP ATTRACTIONS

*** The Waterfront and Colonial Buildings: the hub of historic Singapore.
*** The Ethnic Quarters: Chinatown, Arab Street and Little India.
*** Jurong Bird Park: everything from penguins to toucans in the world's largest aviary.
*** Singapore Zoo: animals who don't have to live behind bars.
*** The Botanic Gardens: tranquil lawns and lakes, virgin rainforest and orchids.
*** The throbbing nightlife of Singapore.

Opposite: *Soaring skyscrapers and traditional shophouses flank the Singapore River in the heart of the city.*

THE GREEN CITY

Modern Singapore tries to strike a balance between progress and conservation, and to foster its image as a 'Garden City' with the establishment and upgrading of parks and protected areas. At the Sungei Buloh Nature Park, for example, mud-flats have been created, with bird hides, sluice gates and a visitor centre. Walkways snaking over the swamps enable visitors to observe mangrove ecology at close range. A national tree planting campaign was launched in 1963 and by 1992 the Parks and Recreation Department was maintaining 746,810 trees – mostly supplied by the Botanic Gardens – and 4268 ha (10,550 acres) of parkland, turfed areas and roadside greenery. There are nature reserves at Bukit Timah, MacRitchie, Peirce, Lower Seletar and Upper Seletar Reservoirs, and Pasir Ris Park.

THE LAND

The Republic of Singapore lies approximately 137km (85 miles) north of the equator off the southernmost tip of **Peninsular Malaysia**, separated from it by the Straits of Johor and from the Indonesian archipelago in the south by the Straits of Singapore. Its territory consists of the island of Singapore and 58 islets of which more than 20 are inhabited. The main island of Singapore is about 42km (26 miles) from west to east and 23km (15 miles) from north to south, with 137km (85 miles) of coastline. About 50% of the island is devoted to residential, commercial and industrial development and some 2% is agricultural land. Approximately one-third of the domestic demand for fresh produce is supplied by high-tech 'agrotechnology parks'. The remainder consists of forest reserves, marshes and other undeveloped tracts.

Climate

With its proximity to the equator, Singapore has a **tropical climate** with a uniformly high average daytime temperature of 31°C (88°F) and a minimum of 23°C (73°F) at night throughout the year. The average relative **humidity** is about 85%, moderated by the prevailing cool sea breeze. Rain falls throughout the year but is heaviest during the **northeast monsoon** season from November to January with an average annual rainfall of 2360mm (93 inches). The driest month is July. February is usually the sunniest month while December has the least sunshine. From April to November, early morning thunderstorms known as 'Sumatras' occur three or four times a month.

Geology and Topography

Three types of rock form the foundation of the island: igneous granite is found in the central and northeast region and sedimentary rocks composed mainly of shale, sandstone and conglomerate in the west, while in the east a veneer of semi-hardened alluvium covers older rocks beneath. The area of granite and other igneous rocks in the centre of the island forms an undulating

Most of Singapore's natural rainforest disappeared long ago to make way for agriculture and urban development on this small, densely populated island. However, a few small pockets of primary vegetation remain and 81ha (200 acres) are protected in the Bukit Timah Nature Reserve, in the hilly centre of the island. Jungle trails wind through the forest beneath the towering canopy, enlivened by shimmering butterflies, exotic birds, monkeys and lemurs.

landscape of rounded **hills** with gentle spurs and valleys, over which rise higher and steeper peaks. The west and southwest regions are furrowed by a series of narrow ridges running in a northwest/southeast direction.

Most of the **coastline** is flat, though cliffs drop down to the sea in a few places, but considerable stretches of the coast have been artificially reclaimed, where embankments have been built and swamps drained. A few small rivers criss-cross the island, of which the largest is **Sungei Seletar**, which is 15km (9 miles) long, and the most prominent is the **Singapore River**. In the built-up areas, however, the valleys are now drained by concrete channels rather than by natural streams.

Plant Life

Singapore, having evolved from a small swampy island clad in tropical rainforest into a thriving city, has lost most of its primary vegetation to urban development. The forests were cut down to make way for agriculture and the rapidly expanding population. Today, only a few pockets of primary vegetation remain in protected areas such as the **Bukit Timah Nature Reserve**. Here, the forest consists mainly of the tropical hardwoods of the dipterocarp family (trees with two-winged seeds), some

---

HILLS OF SINGAPORE

In the hilly central region of the island, the highest point is Bukit Timah at 165m (542ft), followed by Bukit Gombak (139m; 456ft), Bukit Panjang (132m; 433ft), Bukit Batok (106m; 348ft) and Bukit Mandai (88m; 289ft). Mount Faber, with its view over the harbour, rises to 116m (380ft).

Singapore's natural lush vegetation survives in parts of the less developed northern region.

SPIRITS OF THE TREES

In most Asian societies, belief in the spiritual power of trees is common. In Singapore, to witness the dainty yellow blooms of the *Angsana* tree is considered good luck, as it rarely flowers. Locals avoid walking beneath the kapok tree, with its spreading branches, as it is known to be a favourite perching place for ghosts. Long-leaved thorny Kuan Yin plants (named after the Goddess of Mercy) or potted citrus fruits are often found along five-foot ways to keep evil spirits away from the houses. Orange-coloured citrus fruits, such as kumquat, are used as decorations on festive occasions, especially Chinese New Year, to bring prosperity. Mandarin oranges are exchanged as gifts as their Chinese name also means 'gold'. To the Indians, bananas are pleasing to the gods, and their fronds are often found framing temple doorways. For the Chinese, banana trees shelter female spirits and men should take care when passing them, especially after a spell of simultaneous sun and rain (quite common in the tropical climate).

---

of which grow to a towering height of 40m (130ft), forming a green canopy over the other vegetation. Non-dipterocarps like *jelutong*, *jambu* and oaks are also found here. A large number of epiphytes – plants which grow on other plants, usually trees – such as the bird's nest fern and the staghorn fern utilize these forest trees as their hosts.

About 500ha (1250 acres) of **mangrove swamp** prevail along the northern coastline of Kranji and along Sungei Loyang and Sungei Tampines near Pasir Ris. There are patches of marshland in Woodlands and Ulu Pandan and on the northern islands of Pulau Ubin and Pulau Tekong. Along the coast, a variety of grasses, sedges and creepers are found in the sandy areas while *Casuarina*, *Pandanus*, *Calophyllum*, *pong pong*, coconut and yellow sea hibiscus grow further inland.

In the urban and developed areas, about 80% (200 species) of the exotic species planted in public parks, gardens and along roadsides are imported. *Frangipani* was introduced from Mexico, *Caesalpinia* from the West Indies, *Lantana* and *Bougainvillaea* from South America. *Angsana*, the raintree, the yellow flame, the *pong pong* and the *jambu laut* throng the roadsides, functioning as the 'green lungs' of the bustling city and providing shade for pedestrians.

Animal Life

A surprising variety of wildlife is found in this highly urbanized country and new species are still being discovered. In the high canopy of the forest live **vertebrates** such as the flying lemur, two species of squirrel, long-tailed macaques and the flying lizard. The lower canopy is home to shrews, rats, snakes and tree frogs, while lizards, skinks, frogs, snakes and tortoises inhabit the ground. Among the bat species found here are the fruit bat, horseshoe bat, tomb bat, the Malayan flying fox and the Malayan false vampire. Animals such as the tiny mouse-deer, the porcupine and the scaly anteater (or pangolin) survive in Singapore but are rarely seen. Colourful butterflies, moths, beetles and dragonflies abound. A total of 320 **bird** species, including migrants, is currently chronicled.

Aquatic and **insect** life in ponds, streams and reservoirs includes tadpoles, prawns, potamonid crabs, water bugs, dragonfly and damselfly nymphs, and fish such as rasbora, puntius, betta, trichogaster and tilapia. A variety of mussels, barnacles, snails, crabs, mud-lobsters, prawns and mudskippers abound in the brackish water, especially in the mangrove swamps, while the open water is the habitat of glass fish, half-beaks and archer fish. Some tidal **invertebrates** like ghost crabs, bivalves and gastropods are found at low tide on the seashore and high tides bring in the sea slatters. Singapore's offshore waters, albeit murky due to reclamation and dredging activities, support a rich tropical **marine life**. More than 120 species of corals, gorgonians, anemones, clown fish, feathery tube worms, sinister-looking clusters of black sea-urchins, and the occasional poisonous scorpion fish form the reef colony.

> **BIRDS OF SINGAPORE**
>
> A March 1991 national bird census carried out by the Bird Group of the Nature Society of Singapore revealed 12,000 birds in areas like Marina South, Punggol, the Kranji bund and the offshore islands of Sentosa and St John's. Over 300 species have been recorded here. At the bird sanctuary at Sungei Buloh, on the northern coast, migrant birds including terns, egrets, plovers, herons and the Asiatic dowitcher can be observed in the mangrove swamps and ponds.

The park around MacRitchie Reservoir contains areas of primary rainforest and away from the main forest track, popular with joggers, it is rich in wildlife.

HISTORY IN BRIEF
Early History

Early records of Singapore are vague, though it seems to have been a small seaport during the period when the mighty Sumatran **Sri Vijaya Empire** ruled the whole region. According to the 16th-century *Sejarah Melayu*, or 'Malay Annals', **Temasek**, as it was then known, was a flourishing trading post in the 14th century. However, a contemporary Chinese account describes it as a pirate island. It was briefly ruled by the Sumatran prince Parameswara, but invasions by the Thais and Javanese in the 1390s drove him to flee north to Melaka to found the Malay Sultanate there. **Singa Pura** remained undeveloped until the arrival of Thomas Stamford Raffles.

Gazing over the Singapore River up which he sailed in January 1819 stands this white marble statue of Thomas Stamford Raffles, the city's visionary founder.

HISTORICAL CALENDAR		
1819 Thomas Stamford Raffles founds settlement of Singapore and sets up trading post for British East India Company. **1826** Singapore becomes one of the Straits Settlements, together with Penang and Melaka. **1832** Centre of government of Straits Settlements moved to Singapore. **1867** Straits Settlements transferred from East India Company to British colonial administration.	**1942** Singapore captured by Japanese and renamed Syonan. **1945** British regain control of Singapore with surrender of Japanese Imperial Army. **1946** Singapore becomes Crown Colony. **1959** Singapore achieves self-government and holds first general election. Lee Kuan Yew becomes prime minister. **1963** Singapore joins Federation of Malaya, Sarawak and North Borneo to form Malaysia.	**1965** Merger with Malaysia dissolved; Singapore becomes independent republic, and is admitted to United Nations and Commonwealth of Nations. **1967** Association of South-East Asian Nations (ASEAN) established, comprising Singapore, Malaysia, Indonesia, the Philippines and Thailand (Brunei becomes sixth member in 1984). **1990** Lee Kuan Yew resigns as prime minister after 31 years; succeeded by Goh Chok Tong.

Colonial Singapore: the Days of Raffles

During the 18th century, Britain's trade with China was expanding and she saw the need to establish a port of call in this region to refresh and protect her merchant fleet, as well as to thwart the power of the Dutch in the East Indies. A trading post had earlier been established in **Penang** by Francis Light in 1786, but Raffles recognized that a more strategically placed settlement was vital. Then Lieutenant-Governor of Bencoolen in Sumatra, he was given permission to establish such a post and, after surveying nearby islands, landed in Singapore on 29 January 1819.

An administrator of vision with a profound knowledge of Southeast Asia, **Thomas Stamford Raffles** had joined the East India Company as a clerk at the age of 14 and was posted to Penang in 1805 where, unusually for a Company official, he made it his business to learn Malay. He was Lieutenant-Governor of Java while it was under British rule from 1811 to 1816, exercising the free-trade policy which was later to prove so successful in Singapore.

Raffles saw great potential in the swamp-covered but strategically located island. After negotiating a deal with the local rulers, a formal treaty was concluded a month later. Despite scepticism in the British East India

SINGAPORE'S FOUNDING FATHER

Seafaring was undoubtedly in Raffles' blood. The son of a sea-caption, Benjamin Raffles, he was born at sea on 6 July 1771 aboard his father's ship *Ann*. Benjamin Raffles died heavily in debt, so that Thomas was obliged to leave school at 14, but during his years as a clerk in the East India Company he continued to educate himself with fervour. He was an able historian and zoologist and published *A History of Java* in 1817, the year in which he was knighted. In that same year he had suggested to Sir Joseph Banks the establishing of a collection of animals in London. When he returned to live permanently in England in 1824 he and Sir Humphrey Davy founded the Zoological Society of London, of which Raffles became the first president. He died in 1826, two days before his 45th birthday.

Company, the settlement grew rapidly as an entrepôt, serving trade between Europe and East and Southeast Asia. By 1823, Singapore surpassed Penang in importance. Its free-port status attracted traders from all over Asia and from as far afield as the Middle East and the USA. By 1860 the population, a mere 150 in 1819, had grown to 80,792 and consisted primarily of Chinese, followed by Indians and Malays.

The Straits Settlements

In 1826, Singapore, Penang and Melaka were constituted as the 'Straits Settlements'. Initially they were controlled from Calcutta, but in 1832 Singapore, by now the most important of the three ports, became the administrative centre. Their control was transferred from the East India Company to the British government in 1867, when the areas became a Crown Colony.

The advent of steamships in the mid-1860s and the opening of the Suez Canal in 1869 meant that Singapore's importance as an entrepôt became even greater. By the 1870s it was also a major depot for rubber from the plantations proliferating in Malaya. Its trade expanded eightfold between 1873 and 1913.

Modern History

The peace and prosperity of the city was shattered in the early hours of 8 December 1941 when it was bombed by Japanese aircraft. Singapore, which had been considered an impregnable fortress by the British, was occupied by the Japanese on 15 February 1942 and renamed **Syonan** ('Light of the South'). The occupation lasted for three and a half years, during which time great oppression was inflicted on the people and many lives were lost.

After the Japanese surrender in 1945, Singapore came under the British Military Administration until March 1946, when the Straits Settlements, comprised of Penang, Melaka and Singapore, were dissolved. Singapore became a Crown Colony while Penang and Melaka joined the Malayan Union. The country attained self-government in 1959 and the first general election was held to elect 51 representatives to the Legislative Assembly. The People's Action Party (PAP) won a majority of 43 seats and **Lee Kuan Yew** became the first prime minister of Singapore. The PAP formed an uneasy alliance with the communists to fight British colonialism, but conflicts of ideology between the two factions led to a split in 1961. In that year Singapore joined Malaya, and on 16 September 1963 was included in the merger between the Federation of Malaya, Sarawak and North Borneo (now Sabah) to form **Malaysia**. The merger was short-lived: Singapore left Malaysia to become a sovereign, democratic and independent nation on 9 August 1965, and on 22 December that year it became a republic.

After a period of internal conflicts among its immigrant populace, Singapore entered a new epoch of independent survival and development. The 1970s saw political stability and a high rate of economic growth led by the PAP which emerged triumphant from the 1968 general election, setting a pattern for all subsequent elections and holding every seat until 1981. After 31 years in office, Lee Kuan Yew stepped down in 1990 and Goh Chok Tong became the second prime minister of Singapore – one of the great success stories of Asia.

> ### THE FALL OF SINGAPORE
>
> The colonial British in their arrogance (or ignorance) considered Singapore an impregnable fortress, but on 8 December 1941 Japanese aircraft bombed the island. The Imperial Army entered Singapore not from the sea, as anticipated, but through the 'back door', Malaya. The occupying force moved inland through Ulu Pandan, Pasir Panjang, Bukit Timah, Seletar and Paya Lebar. The defenders were out-manoeuvred and outnumbered. Kent Ridge Park, Alexandra Hospital and Labrador Park saw the fiercest battles, which included hand-to-hand combat with the British troops aided by their harbour guns turned inland. Despite a show of bravery by the troops and an order to 'fight it to the end', General Arthur Percival had no choice but to sign a truce with General Tomoyuki Yamashita, the commander of the Japanese army, in the Ford Factory boardroom at 19:50 on 15 February 1942. Singapore had fallen after only seven days of fighting.

*Singapore in the 1890s: Boat Quay and the Singapore River crowded with boats (**opposite**) and nutmeg plantations lining Orchard Road (**left**).*

The guiding spirit of modern Singapore began his professional life as a lawyer before manoeuvring his way into politics. He was sworn into office as the country's first prime minister on 5 June 1959. A speech he made in 1968 revealed his ambition as a politician: 'I take comfort from the fact that even in the dark ages there were places like Venice which shone out and lit the way back into the Renaissance. And perhaps that is the role we may be asked to play. I would like to believe that we can be the sparking plug for a great deal of co-operative endeavour . . . and economic and social well-being.'

The PAP under his leadership has so far won all the general elections since 1959. In his 31-year rule of Singapore he led the country through a difficult period of political unrest and turned it into one of the most affluent countries in the world – the 'Tiger of Asia'.

Betting on horses and entering lotteries are the only legal forms of gambling in Singapore, and Singaporeans spend about $1 billion on lottery tickets each year. They are great believers in lucky numbers and tend to crowd around after a car crash, not ghoulishly to peer at the victims, but to note down the cars' registration numbers for future use.

GOVERNMENT AND ECONOMY

Whilst some criticisms have been hurled from the outside world at Singapore's seemingly strict régime, it is hard to find fault with a government that has transformed and meticulously moulded the country into an almost utopian state. Today Singapore boasts a booming economy, an educated populace enjoying high employment and a low crime rate, in addition to political stability and a standard of living that is among the highest in Asia.

GOVERNMENT

Singapore is a republic with a parliamentary system of government based on universal adult suffrage. Voting is compulsory for all citizens above the age of 21. The head of state is the **president**, who is elected by the people every six years, and who selects his cabinet on the advice of the **prime minister**. The administration of the government devolves upon the cabinet headed by the prime minister, who is appointed by the president.

The unicameral **parliament** consists of 81 members elected by secret ballot in single member constituencies and group representative constituencies (GRCs), each electing four members of a single party, of which one must come from an ethnic minority community. The parliament serves a minimum of five years. Since March 1990, the president has been able to appoint up to six people who are not members of the ruling party as nominated members (NMPs) to provide for a wider representation of views in parliament. In addition, four non-constituency members of parliament (NCMPs), inclusive of opposition members, are elected to represent opposition political parties. The People's Action Party (PAP) has been in power since 1959, when Lee Kuan Yew became the country's first prime minister.

POLICIES

Singapore's **legal system** is based on the British judiciary system. The Supreme Court, consisting of the High Court, Court of Appeal and Court of Criminal Appeal, is

The classical façade of the Supreme Court, one of the most imposing monuments of the colonial era, completed in 1939.

presided over by the chief justice and other judges appointed by the president. The Subordinate Courts consist of District Courts, Magistrates' Courts, Juvenile Courts, Coroners' Courts and Small Claim Tribunals. The Shariah is a religious court framed by Islamic law with jurisdiction over domestic disputes between Muslims.

Defence and Security

Intent on protecting its independence, Singapore maintains a strong, well-equipped defence force of 55,500 servicemen. There are extensive military installations along its north and west coasts, the areas that proved vulnerable to the Japanese in 1941. All able-bodied male citizens of Singapore and permanent residents, who have reached the age of 18 or completed their pre-university education, are conscripted into the Singapore Defence Force for full-time service lasting two or two-and-a-half years, depending on the rank attained. After fulfilling their national service requirement, they are liable for reservist training for up to 40 days a year up to the age of 45 for non-commissioned officers and 55 for commissioned officers.

Housing and Urban Redevelopment

The public housing programme and urban redevelopment in Singapore is much celebrated. The function of the Urban Redevelopment Authority (URA) is to eradicate slums in urban areas through careful city

Blocks of flats on one of Singapore's model housing estates.

Opposite: *Cavenagh Bridge links the colonial core of the city with the business district.*

planning with modern high-rise office buildings, smart shopping complexes and hotels, supported by a well-planned infrastructure. The **Housing Development Board** (HDB) is responsible for planning and building affordable quality housing and almost 87% of the people are now housed in HDB flats. These housing schemes are enhanced by improved public facilities, recreational areas and parks.

Central Narcotics Bureau

Singapore takes a stringent stand over drug abuse. The CNB was set up to combat drug abuse and trafficking, liaising closely with the police and customs departments. Its various means of enforcement are backed by tough legislation; the misuse and trafficking of heroin or cocaine over a prescribed very small amount carries the **death penalty**. Addicts are put through compulsory treatment and rehabilitation programmes, while educational resources highlight the dangers of drug abuse. An independent voluntary organization, the Singapore Anti-Narcotics Association, administers preventive educational programmes and gives support and counselling to drug-abusers.

The Corrupt Practices Investigation Bureau

The CPIB is an independent body which investigates and acts as a deterrent against corruption in both the public and private sectors. Established in 1952, it answers directly to the prime minister. As a preventive measure, the bureau researches into work procedures of corruption-prone departments and public bodies to isolate any existing administrative weakness. It also gives lectures to recruits in the public service whose duties might expose them to the temptation of bribery and corruption.

TRADE AND INDUSTRY

Singapore's advantageous geographical position contributes to its importance as a world centre for commerce and industry. Blessed with a **natural deep harbour** on one of the busiest trade routes between West and East, it has a market economy based on the principle of free enterprise.

Its former role as an entrepôt is diminishing. Emphasis is now placed on **manufacturing** and **finance** and **business services**, which are the greatest contributors to its GDP, with growth reaching 6% in 1993 and 7% in 1994. The Economic Development Board spearheads the country's industrialization policy through the promotion of investment in manufacturing and the encouragement of business operations. In addition, the Singapore Trade Development Board was set up in 1983 as a trade promotion agency to develop and expand **international trade**. Despite rapid economic growth, inflation has remained low (2.4% in 1993).

The manufacturing sector concentrates on electronic products and components, while machinery, industrial chemicals, paints, pharmaceuticals, food, printing and publishing are also major contributors.

Finance and Investment

Its traditional role as an entrepôt in the region, backed by its political and economic stability and a well-developed communication and financial infrastructure, has contributed to Singapore's key position as an international financial and banking centre, notably for the Asia-Pacific region. It has continued to attract considerable **foreign investment**, reaching a record high of S$3.5 billion investment commitments in 1992. To lure foreign investors, there are attractive incentives such as tax concessions and unrestricted repatriation or importation of capital, profits, dividends and royalties. Blessed with a perceptive government, an educated and industrious population and a competent constitution, Singapore has blazed a trail towards its desired status as a developed country.

TOURISM

Tourism is fast becoming a major contributor to Singapore's growing economy. The Singapore Tourist Promotion Board (STPB), formed in 1964, aims to attract 6.8 million visitors annually by 1995, up 10% from 1992. The average length of stay in Singapore is 3.7 days, but it is committed to change its 'shop till you drop', stopover image and entice visitors to stay longer. A S$1 billion tourist facilities programme is in progress, and an earnest conservation project was launched in the 1980s, restoring landmarks such as Raffles Hotel, Chinatown and Little India.

STPB is also aggressively promoting Singapore as a world-class convention and exhibition centre: a S$13 million programme, 'Meet in Singapore 1995', has been launched to coincide with the unveiling of the S$2 billion Suntech City – Singapore International Convention and Exhibition Centre.

TRANSPORT

Singapore owes its reputation as the hub of international communications and transportation to its geographical location and its harbour. Its infrastructural facilities are amongst the most developed in the world.

Air Communication

As a major airport, according to a 1993 report, Singapore has connections to 113 cities in 54 countries, served by 63 airlines which make a total of 2600 flights each week. Further air service agreements are under negotiation with other countries. In the previous year, 719,005 tonnes of cargo were handled at Changi Airport by Singapore Air Terminal Services and Changi International Airport Services.

Shipping

In terms of shipping tonnage, Singapore ranks as the busiest **port** in the world, with up to 700 ships in its harbour at any one time. More than 92,000 vessels called at the port in 1993, carrying a total of 623.8 million gross registered tons. More than 600 shipping lines with links to 800 ports use Singapore as a global distribution port. It is also the world's top bunkering port and third largest **oil refining** centre, with the presence of major oil companies like Shell, Caltex, Esso, British Petroleum and

A network of modern expressways carries traffic to all parts of the island.

Mobil. The port is managed by the Port Authority of Singapore which provides a range of services including cargo handling, distribution, warehousing, bunkering and ship supplies, with 24-hour security, environmental control and fire-fighting services.

Loading containers in the world's busiest port.

Free Trade Zones

There are six free trade zones for seaborne cargo and one for air cargo at Singapore Changi Airport. Goods stored within these zones enjoy custom-free facilities until they are released into the market. They can also be processed and re-exported with minimum customs formalities.

Land Transport

The main priority in Singapore's limited area is the smooth flow of traffic. This is achieved by methodical town planning with a comprehensive network of roads, expressways and flyovers and an effective public transport system that integrates the **Mass Rapid Transport** (MRT) and the **bus** services. Restricted zones are imposed in the **Central Business District** during peak hours and public holidays, when drivers entering the controlled zones are liable to pay a surcharge. Public transport in Singapore is efficient and reliable and getting around on the island is inexpensive and easy.

CRUISE HUB OF ASIA

With its strategic geographical position and natural deep harbour, now enhanced by the opening of the new S$50 million purpose-built Singapore Cruise Centre at the World Trade Centre, Singapore is poised to be the new gateway for cruises to exotic destinations in South-east Asia. As travellers have begun to look beyond the Caribbean and Mediterranean, Singapore's cruise industry has been growing, including fly-cruise via its international airport. With undeniably excellent amenities at the new Cruise Centre, it now seems set to be a major port of call for regular back-to-back cruise series by the principal liners.

**DOS AND DON'TS
IN MALAY SOCIETY**

The Malays are steeped in
tradition and custom and it is
advisable to bear this in mind
when meeting them.
•Always remove your shoes
and leave them outside
before entering a Malay
home. Dirt from shoes not
only brings bad luck but is
unhygienic as Malays
traditionally sit on the floor.
•A man should not shake
hands with an adult female in
a traditional family: just
acknowledge her with a smile
and a slight nod of the head.
Malays forbid bodily contact
between unmarried men and
women.
•Always use your right hand
to eat or to hand things to
others, as left hands are for
more 'basic' purposes only.
•It is taboo and impolite to
touch the heads of adult
Malays.
•It is against Islamic law to
eat pork or drink alcohol, so
do not bring such gifts to a
Malay home.
•When sitting on the floor,
do not stretch your legs
towards anyone. Men should
sit cross-legged and women
should fold their legs to the
right.

THE PEOPLE

Singapore's geographical position and commercial
success were major influences on the composition of its
population. After its founding by Sir Stamford Raffles,
the small sea town was quickly established as a
flourishing trading post. It became a magnet for
migrants and merchants from China, the Indian sub-
continent, Indonesia, the Malay Peninsula and the
Middle East. They came in search of a better place to
settle down, lured by the riches of the land and bringing
with them their own cultures, languages, customs and
festivals. Through intermarriage and integration, these
diverse human 'ingredients' have merged into the multi-
faceted society that is unique to Singapore today: a
young nation with a vibrant and diverse cultural
heritage.

Early Immigrants

Sailing up the Singapore River in 1819, Raffles found a
small settlement of about 150 people along its banks. As
the island began to turn into a thriving port, encouraged
by its free trade policy, the first wave of immigration
consisted of Malays and Chinese from the older, Dutch-
ruled settlement of Melaka. Other major groups of
immigrants were the Javanese, Bugis and Balinese who
were mainly traders and labourers. Drawn together by
their cultural similarities and the common bond of Islam,

*Traditions abound in ultra-
modern Singaporean
society: citrus plants flank
an entrance to ward off evil
spirits (**right**) and fortune-
tellers thrive (**opposite**).*

the Indonesians intermarried with the indigenous Malays and at first formed the largest group: in 1824 the Malays made up 60% of the population, with 31% Chinese and 7% Indians. But by 1830 the Chinese had become the largest ethnic component of the population. Singapore was to become the most cosmopolitan city in Asia by the end of the 19th century. Apart from the major ethnic groups, Jews, Eurasians, Europeans and Armenians also settled there. Today, the population consists of 78% Chinese, 14% Malays, 7% Indians and 1% Eurasians or of other descent, making a total of 2.8 million.

The Chinese

Of Singapore's 150 inhabitants in 1819, 30 were Chinese farmers engaged in pepper and gambier cultivation. But the new trading opportunities soon began to attract a continuous stream of Chinese immigrants. By the mid-19th century, Chinese immigration was well organized. Most arrived as indentured labourers. Having incurred heavy debts to pay for their passage, they were inevitably exploited as forced labour by their sponsors, until the indenture system was abolished in 1914. As foreigners in a strange land without their families, many sought the protection of the various Chinese clan associations and secret societies. These rival allegiances militated against integration among the Chinese, as did their diverse dialects and sub-cultures. But as they became more settled their families began to join them, encouraged by official policy.

By 1912 the Chinese population had risen to 250,000 in number. The Hokkiens dominated the commercial scene from the beginning, followed closely by the Teochews, while the Cantonese were mostly farmers, artisans, carpenters, tailors and goldsmiths. The motives of the Chinese for leaving their poverty-stricken and war-torn homeland were purely economic, and they continued to pledge their loyalty to their motherland. Today the Chinese form the largest ethnic group of Singapore's population, and the economy of the country

CHINESE HOROSCOPES

When Buddha summoned all the animals before his departure from earth, only 12 turned up to bid him farewell and as a reward he named a year after each, in order of their arrival. First came the Rat, then the Ox, Tiger, Rabbit, Dragon, Snake, Horse, Sheep, Monkey, Rooster, Dog and finally, the Boar. The Chinese believe that the animal ruling the year of your birth exercises a profound influence on your life. The Chinese lunar calendar is the longest chronological record in history: it dates back to 2637 BC during the reign of Emperor Huang Ti. It takes 60 years to complete a cycle, as each animal sign is combined with each of the five main elements: Wood, ruled by the planet Jupiter; Fire by Mars; Earth by Saturn; Metal or Gold by Venus; and Water by Mercury. These in turn are further split into the opposing poles of the positive (yin) and the negative (yang).

One of the many faces of Singapore: 7% of the population is of Indian extraction.

is their stronghold. They fervently preserve their traditions and customs and Chinatown still bears witness to the various colourful and ancient cultures the Chinese brought with them.

The Indians

Indians began to arrive in Singapore as soon as the island was established as a British trading post. Raffles brought with him an entourage of 120 Indian soldiers and several assistants from Penang. The promise of free trade and ample opportunities for employment drew Indians from Penang, India and Sri Lanka seeking work as civil servants, teachers, technicians and traders. When the British decided to make Singapore a penal station in 1823, several hundred Indian prisoners were brought in as convict labourers to build government offices and other parts of the new colony's infrastructure. Examples of their work are St Andrew's Cathedral, Sri Mariamman Temple and the Istana. Indentured labourers were imported from southern India to build roads, railways, bridges, canals and wharves. The indenture system was eventually banned in 1910 after much public protest.

TYING THE KNOT

In 1995, Chap Goh Meh, the last day of the Lunar New Year celebrations, fell on 14 February – St Valentine's Day. The multicultural Singaporeans rushed to take advantage of the coincidence: over 1000 couples were married on this doubly auspicious day.

A young devotee at the Sri Mariamman Temple, Singapore's oldest and largest Hindu temple.
Opposite: *Intriguing foodstuffs line the five-foot way in front of this Chinatown shop.*

Indians continued to flood in until immigration controls were strictly imposed in the early 1950s.

Although almost all major Indian ethnic groups are represented in Singapore, about 80% are from southern India. They maintain a strong bond with their native land as is evident in the preservation and practice of their religion, customs and festivals. Little India is 'a home from home' for the Indian community.

The Islamic Community

The prospect of a more prosperous life drew Singapore's neighbours to its shores as early immigrants. From the Malay Peninsula came the Malays, from Indonesia, the Sumatrans, Javanese, Bugis and the Balinese. Despite regional differences in cultures and dialects, the Muslim community, including the Arabs who mainly arrived later as merchants, integrated well. Their traditional cultures and customs are still evident today in the Islamic quarter in Arab Street.

Language

The national language of Singapore is Malay, while English is the language of administration and commerce. Tamil and Chinese are also official languages. Mandarin is increasingly encouraged as the lingua franca for the Chinese in place of dialects like Hokkien, Teochew, Cantonese, Hakka, Hainanese and Foochow. Among the Indian community, apart from Tamil, other languages spoken are Malayalam, Punjabi, Telegu, Hindi and Bengali. Most of the literate population is bi-lingual, and domestically English and Mandarin are the most commonly used languages. In parliamentary debates, members may speak in Malay, Mandarin, Tamil or English and simultaneous oral translations are provided.

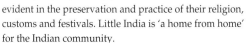

ONE KIND LANGUAGE, CATCH NO BALL!

The multi-racial community of Singapore has evolved its own unique vernacular, called Singlish. A mixture of English and local dialects, it is not unlike pidgin English:

Lah Used at the end of a sentence to add emphasis.
One kind Describes a type of place or person: 'He is one kind lah.'
Go fly kite Get lost.
Catch no ball Cannot understand.
Kiasu Afraid to lose out (Singaporeans hate missing out on things, especially if they have paid for them.)
Can or not? Asking a favour: 'Go with me, can or not?'
Ang mo Any Caucasian.
Kay poh A busybody or chatterbox.
Alamah Expression of shock or surprise.
Aiyah Exasperation or frustration: 'Aiyah, so hot one!'
Wah Incredibly: 'Wah! she is so pretty.'
Go-stan To go astern or reverse (as in a car).

RELIGION

With such a diverse population, most major religions are represented in Singapore. Among the Chinese community, **Buddhism** and **Taoism** are the most popular while ancestor worship and other Chinese sects also have their adherents. Buddhists and Taoists constituted 54% of the population at the time of the 1990 census. **Islam** is the official religion of the Malays, but there are also converts among the Indian, Chinese and other communities, and Muslims make up 15% of the population. **Christians** represent 12.5% of Singapore society (with Protestants outnumbering Roman Catholics), and of these 88% are Chinese. Some 4% of Singaporeans are **Hindus**, almost all Indian.

FESTIVALS

Every ethnic group in Singapore has its own festivals, mostly related to its religion. Almost every month of the year sees a celebration of some form or other, bringing a visual feast of colour, pomp and ceremony which is enjoyed by the whole population. In a peaceful and harmonious society, Singaporeans respect and celebrate one another's festivals with relish.

Chinese Festivals

The most vibrant and colourful festival in the Chinese calendar is the **Lunar New Year**, when the whole of Chinatown is ablaze with lights from ceremonial red

lanterns, and the streets are bedecked with traditional decorations mainly in red, the colour of good luck. The Singapore River is the venue for colourful stalls selling food, handicrafts and New Year souvenirs to bring luck. The celebration starts with family reunion dinner on New Year's Eve, followed by open-house over the next few days. It is a time for forgiveness and for settling old debts. The festival lasts for 15 days and concludes with a big celebration called **Chap Goh Mei**.

The seventh month of the lunar year is devoted to the **Festival of the Hungry Ghosts**, during which the gates of hell are thrown open and the spirits of the dead are released on 'parole' to roam the earth. Food, prayers, incense and 'hell money' are offered to appease the spirits. Celebratory dinners are held as well as performances of Chinese street operas or *wayang*. No marriages or betrothals will be conducted during this month, or dangerous journeys, such as sea voyages, embarked on.

The **Moon Cake** or **Mid-Autumn Festival** commemorates the patriot Zhu Yuan Zhang, who plotted to overthrow the tyrannical rule of the Yuan dynasty in the 14th century, and is said to have passed his plans to his fellow rebels hidden in mooncakes. Hence today, these moon-shaped pastries with sweet fillings of red bean and lotus seed paste are exchanged as gifts. Lanterns were also used to send signals during the rebellion, so lanterns of all shapes and sizes are carried in processions. In Singapore the Chinese Garden is the special venue for this most beautiful of all the Chinese festivals.

*Spectacular Chinese festivals: huge joss-sticks are burned during the Festival of the Hungry Ghosts (**above**), while Chinatown blazes with red and gold, the colours of good luck, for the Lunar New Year celebrations (**opposite**).*

RELIGIOUS TOLERANCE

As a strictly secular state, Singapore is anxious to preserve its ethnic harmony by avoiding any hint of fundamentalism or the mixing of religion with politics. The Maintenance of Religious Harmony Act, introduced in 1988, banned attempts by adherents of any one faith to convert others, and barred the teaching of religion in schools.

DRAGON BOAT FESTIVAL

This festival falls on the fifth day of the fifth lunar month (in June) to commemorate the death of Qu Yuan, a Chinese poet and statesman of the 4th century BC, who drowned himself in protest against political corruption. Fishermen raced in their boats to save him but they were too late. The people made glutinous rice dumplings with savoury meat fillings wrapped in bamboo leaves called *bah chang* and threw them in the river to distract the fish from eating his body. Since then, on the anniversary of his death, this gesture has been re-enacted with a boat race – now called 'The World Invitational Dragon Boat Race' – in Marina Bay, in which teams from all over the world compete. Stalls around the bay sell rice dumplings and souvenirs.

Insistent drum-beats urge on the competitors in the annual Dragon Boat Race in Marina Bay.

Islamic Festivals

In the Muslim community **Hari Raya Puasa** marks the end of the fasting month of Ramadan. The festival begins with morning prayers in the mosque, followed by a thanksgiving feast. It is a time for forgiveness and a strengthening of bonds in the community. New clothes are donned, houses decorated and friends of all races are invited to share this joyous occasion. The Malay area of Geylang is illuminated to welcome the festive season.

Hari Raya Haji is the celebration of the conclusion of the Haj pilgrimage to Mecca, at which pilgrims are given the title of Haji (for men) or Hajjah (for women). Goats or buffaloes are sacrificed and the meat distributed to the poor.

Indian Festivals

Deepavali celebrates the victory of good over evil, symbolized by the legendary slaying of the oppressive Narakasura by Lord Krishna. It marks the beginning of the Indian New Year, and for the business community it is a time for settling debts. It is also believed that the souls of departed relatives descend to earth during this festival, and oil lamps are lit to guide them. Like the New Year festivals of the Chinese and Muslims, it is celebrated with 'open-house' visits among friends of all races. Little India's temples and streets are decorated with spectacular displays of lights, tinsel and garlands.

The most dramatic Indian festival is **Thaipusam**. Devotees go through a strict and careful spiritual preparation before embarking on a ritual journey of penitential self-mutilation. They pierce their bodies with metal hooks supporting heavy structures called *kavadis* decorated with peacock feathers and offerings. In their tranced state, not a

Extraordinary acts of religious devotion are undergone during the Hindu festival of Thaipusam, when tranced penitents pierce their flesh with skewers and hooks supporting heavy kavadis *decorated with flowers and peacock feathers.*

drop of blood is shed as they process from the Sri Srinivasa Perumal Temple in Serangoon Road to the Sri Thandayuthapani Temple in Tank Road.

Another spectacular festival is **Thimithi**, the fire-walking ceremony, held at the Sri Mariamman Temple in South Bridge Road. Devotees defy all sense of pain by walking across a bed of burning coals without so much as a flinch or a blister to show for their ordeal.

Vesak

The festival celebrated with great ceremonial ritual by Buddhists is **Vesak Day**, which commemorates the birth and enlightenment of Buddha and his entry into Nirvana.

The day starts with chanting of the sutras by saffron-clad monks, while devotees visit the temples to pray and meditate and to make offerings. Acts of generosity known as *dana* are observed by Buddhist organizations and temples. These include the freeing of caged birds and animals, visiting and giving alms to the poor and needy, while some Buddhist youths organize mass blood donation at hospitals. The celebration concludes with a candlelit procession through the streets. Observers as well as devotees are welcome to join in the celebration at Buddhist temples.

CHINGAY SINGAPORE

This is the biggest and most spectacular street parade on the island, in which participants from all over the world take part. Chingay means 'the art of mas-querading' and was once a purely Chinese procession, but Singapore's other cultural groups characteristically joined in. Nowadays it is a glamorous showcase of international cultures from countries like USA, Britain, New Zealand, Malaysia, Japan, the Philippines, Taiwan, Seychelles and many more. It is held annually on the first Saturday of the Lunar New Year celebrations in Orchard Road, in the heart of the shopping and entertainment district of Singapore. It attracts over 100,000 spectators, both locals and tourists, and is shown live on Singapore Television.

Passengers may not carry the malodorous durian on board the MRT.

WHAT TO DRINK IN SINGAPORE

Apart from water, which is perfectly safe to drink in Singapore (and therefore also safe as ice in drinks) thirst-quenchers in the tropical heat include:

Fruit juice: many varieties are available freshly squeezed everywhere you go.

Tea: the perfect complement to Chinese food.

Beer: the local brews are Tiger and Anchor. Western beers are widely available. Other local favourites are Malay *ayer bandung* (made with rose syrup and condensed milk) and soya bean milk. Wines, spirits and fizzy soft drinks are all easily available.

FOOD AND DRINK

To describe Singapore as a gourmet's paradise is not an exaggeration. It is a country where serious eating is a favourite pastime. Food centres and hawker stalls, which serve mostly fresh local fare, are very inexpensive, and what they lack in decor (not to mention air-conditioning) they make up for in local colour. Local dishes are a unique blend of **Malay**, **Indian**, **Chinese** and **Nonya** cuisines. It is common practice to pay for your food and drinks when they are served. You can order from any stall as seats are shared between the vendors. Expect to pay more for food in air-conditioned restaurants, while hotel restaurants can be quite expensive. No smoking is allowed in any indoor restaurants in Singapore, though there is no restriction in alfresco eating-places.

Chinese Food

Chinese cuisine plays a leading role on the gastronomic stage of Singapore. Although most of the Chinese population originated from Fukien, Chinese food in Singapore is largely **Cantonese** in style. **Beijing** and spicy **Szechuan** dishes are also gaining in popularity, while the **Hainanese** are famous for their chicken rice.

In Chinese society, eating is more than the mere consumption of food. A Chinese banquet is a visual feast of colours and elaborate garnishes, and ingredients are

Chilli crab, a local favourite, is among the temptations offered at this night market stall.

Hawker stalls outside the ornate Lau Pa Sat Festival Market.

combined to ensure harmony between the *yin* and *yang* qualities of the food. On festive occasions food is chosen for its symbolic associations. For example, noodles are a compulsory dish at birthdays to symbolize longevity, oysters bring good fortune to the Cantonese as their name also means 'good things' or 'business', and fish signifies prosperity.

Indian Food

Cuisines from the Indian sub-continent are well represented in Singapore. There is a wide choice of dishes, from fiery **southern Indian** curries enriched with coconut milk to creamy yoghurt-based dishes from the **Punjab**. Little India is noted for its vegetarian restaurants, while the more adventurous might want to sample the renowned fish-head curry, cooked with okra and brinjals and served with pickles and rice heaped high on a banana leaf. **Indian Muslims** serve their own speciality of *nasi biryani*, a saffron rice dish with spicy chicken or mutton, and *murtabak*, unleavened bread with minced meat and onions.

Malay/Indonesian Food

Malay food is spicy without necessarily being chilli hot, although this fiery spice is used in most dishes. It makes liberal use of coconut and local spices and sometimes borrows subtly from Indian cooking, as is evident in its

Laksa, a Nonya speciality, forms the centrepiece of this feast.

Korma dishes of mild chicken curry and *nasik minyak*, rice cooked with spices and ghee. **Peanut sauce** plays a vital part in dishes like *gado gado*, an Indonesian salad of lettuce, bean sprouts and fried bean curd topped with peanut sauce. **Satay**, skewers of meat grilled over charcoal, served with raw onions, cucumber and ketupat (coconut rice cubes) are also accompanied by peanut sauce, as is *tauhu goreng*, fried bean curd stuffed with shredded raw vegetables. *Sambal belachan*, shrimp paste with chilli and lime, is eaten with raw vegetables or rice. If you are eating in a group it would be fun to try the *rijstaffel*, a Dutch-Indonesian meal of rice and spicy dishes served in ten or twelve courses.

Malay and Indian foods are traditionally eaten with the fingertips of the right hand, but restaurants do provide eating implements for the uninitiated.

Nonya Food

Nonya or Peranakan food is a blend of Malay and Chinese cooking, utilizing local ingredients to produce one of the most popular and exquisite cuisines of the region. Coconut, tamarind, lemon grass, shrimp paste and chilli form the basis of most of its dishes. A famous Nonya dish is *laksa* (actually Indian in origin), rice vermicelli served in coconut milk and garnished with prawns, chicken and bean sprouts.

Other Cuisines

With its cosmopolitan society, visitors to Singapore are spoilt for choice of international cuisines. From other Asian countries come Japanese, Thai, Korean, Vietnamese and Mongolian restaurants, while virtually all types of western food are served here.

BEAN CURD

Bean curd is a popular item on Chinese menus. It is eaten as an alternative to meat by many health-watchers and vegetarians as it has twice as much protein weight for weight, minus the fat. Its origin is known to date back 2000 years to the Han Dynasty when it was invented by a Taoist prince.

Bean curd is made from soya beans which are processed by soaking, grinding, boiling and coagulating into a jelly-like ivory curd. Its versatility makes it a favourite ingredient amongst Chinese chefs, who have mastered the art of cooking the curd to emulate the texture and appearance of meat. It is delicious in any shape or form, be it as drink, stir-fry, in soup or steamed.

ARTS AND ENTERTAINMENT

Singapore's juxtaposition of Eastern and Western culture has produced a new breed of artists whose work incorporates the traditions of both as well as contemporary influences.

National Arts Council

The NAC, established in 1991 to 'develop Singapore into a vibrant global city for the arts', provides funds and support for groups and activities. It organizes festivals and other events and co-ordinates exchange programmes with other ASEAN countries. The **Festival of Arts** is a major biennial event, usually held in June, featuring internationally renowned and outstanding home-grown talents in a wide range of Asian and Western programmes. The **Festival of Asian Performing Arts** highlights the cultural heritage of Asia in addition to the vibrant traditions of Singapore's own ethnic communities.

Young People's Theatre is an annual event designed to encourage young Singaporeans to appreciate the performing arts and to foster budding playwrights and actors.

Several art galleries hold exhibitions throughout the year, including the **National Museum and Art Gallery**, the **Empress Place Museum**, and private galleries like

Gleaming office buildings soar skywards in Raffles Place.

GOH SOON TIOE – ONE GREAT SYMPHONY

This Sumatran-born maestro carved a name for himself in the history of classical music in Singapore for over three decades from the 1950s. He was a performer, impresario, teacher and conductor and was a leading light in the development of music in Singapore. In the 1930s he studied in Barcelona under two great masters, the guitarist Andres Segovia and the violinist Francisco Costa. He devoted his life to teaching music and many of his students achieved renown. Amongst them are luminaries such as Choo Hoey, the present resident conductor of the Singapore Symphony Orchestra, Melvyn Tan the pianist, Margaret Tan, Seow Yit Kin and the child prodigy, Lee Pan Hon, dubbed 'Wonder Boy'. Pan Hon, from Sago Lane in Chinatown, started playing a violin made by his father when he was only five. Amazed that such a young boy who could not read music could play so well by ear, Goh took him under his wing. Today, Pan Hon is leader of the Hallé Orchestra in Manchester, England. Goh died on 27 February 1982 but his music plays on through his students and his daughters, who are continuing his great work teaching music in Singapore today.

Many traditional shophouses in Chinatown disappeared during the 1960s and 70s to make way for new building, but these days those that escaped demolition are now being lovingly restored to their former ornate glory.

Art Base, 78 Shenton Way; **Art Focus** at Centrepoint, Orchard Road; the **Della Butcher Gallery**, 39A Cuppage Terrace; and the **Clifford Galleries** at the Clifford Centre.

For further information, contact the National Arts Council, 460 Alexandra Road, 35th Storey PSA Building, Singapore 0511, tel 270 0722, fax 273 6880/6862.

Architecture

Singapore's architecture is as diverse in style as in age. Ranks of ultra-modern tinted glass-clad skyscrapers, sprouting up to dizzy heights, are punctuated by very grand and handsome edifices from the colonial era. Among the ethnic quarters of Little India, Arab Street and Chinatown are old shophouses with five-foot ways, remnants of the thriving bazaars of days gone by, where little has changed in the manner of trade. Where these buildings survive they are now being painstakingly restored by the government as part of its heritage conservation programme.

ENTERTAINMENT

Singapore comes alive when night falls, with entertainments galore to amuse even the most discerning visitor. The city boasts a plethora of night spots from discos, jazz clubs, karaoke bars and pubs to theatres, cinemas and cultural shows.

For the young and young-at-heart there are many night clubs and discos to choose from. For a pulsating atmosphere and ear-splitting music, head for the **Warehouse** at River View Hotel, 382 Havelock Road; **Zouk** on Jiak Kim Street, **Top Ten** at 400 Orchard Road; **Fire Discotheque** at 150 Orchard Road; and **Hard Rock**

CINEMA

Singapore has more than 50 cinemas, and new films arrive here very quickly. Less mainstream, 'alternative' and classic movies are screened at the Picturehouse in Dhoby Ghaut and Jade Classics in Beach Road. Details are listed in the daily press. All the cinemas are air-conditioned.

This beautiful traditional house in Petain Road, Little India, shows a typical adoption of European styles with its Corinthian columns, louvred windows and lavish use of decorative tiles.

Café at 50 Cuscaden Road.

Jazz lovers can visit **Harry's Quayside Café** at Boat Quay; the **Bar and Billiard Room** at Raffles Hotel Arcade; **Saxophone Bar and Restaurant** at 23 Cuppage Road; and **Sparks** at 391 Orchard Road.

For a uniquely Singaporean cabaret act, try the **Boom Boom Room** at Bugis Village. The show starts at 23:00 with a non-stop routine of 'send-ups' starring Kumar, the transvestite compère who mimes to pop songs in a splendid array of gowns, and whose repertoire of very risqué humour, told in 'Singlish', will keep you entertained all night. If you do not wish to be dragged on stage to participate – the jokes will be at your expense – avoid the front seats.

KARAOKE

The craze that has swept Singapore originated in Japan and is prevalent in most clubs and restaurants, and even on board Chinese junks during pleasure cruises. The Japanese word karaoke loosely translates as 'without orchestra' and it is a diversion which you either become addicted to or handle with trepidation. Umpteen 'murders' are regularly committed in karaoke lounges as those under the illusion that they can sing kill popular songs, belting out the words displayed on the monitor screens. Amongst many other places, the Singsation at the Plaza Hotel on Beach Road has 19 karaoke rooms where enthusiasts can indulge their fantasies by singing in a spaceship or a car, as if they were at a drive-in.

Elaborate costumes and makeup, dramatic movement and music make Chinese street opera a spectacular entertainment.

At Clarke Quay there is a host of pubs, restaurants and discos, including **Party Doll**, where you can dance to music from the 1950s and 60s.

For indigenous cultural shows, spend an evening at the **Cockpit Hotel** on Oxley Rise, the **Mandarin Hotel** on Orchard Road or the **Singa Inn Seafood Restaurant** on East Coast Parkway. There are nightly performances of the lion dance and other Chinese, Malay and Indian dances from Singapore and its Southeast Asian neighbours.

During the Festival of the Hungry Ghosts in August and September, and for other festivals and temple celebrations, **Chinese operas** are performed on makeshift stages at street corners. For details of these performances, contact the Singapore Tourist Information Service (see page 122).

The Singapore Symphony Orchestra

Established in 1979, the SSO is Singapore's only professional orchestra. Under the direction of its resident conductor, Choo Hoey, it gives regular concerts of music from the Baroque to the 20th century at the **Victoria Concert Hall** and at various open-air venues. It has accompanied many distinguished soloists including Luciano Pavarotti and Placido Domingo.

Theatre

The theatre scene in Singapore is very cosmopolitan, and venues like the **Drama Centre** in Canning Rise, the **Victoria Theatre** in Empress Place, the **Substation** in Armenian Street, the **Black Box** (of TheatreWorks) in Canning Park, **Singapore Indoor Stadium** and the **Harbour Pavilion** at the World Trade Centre stage local as well as international productions of plays, musicals and ballets. Details of performances can be obtained from local newspapers or from the individual venues.

ALFRESCO OPERA

Chinese opera, or *wayang*, is often performed at street corners on makeshift stages during festivals such as Yu Lan Jie, the Festival of the Hungry Ghosts, Chinese New Year or clan birthdays. The actors, lavishly plastered with layers of make-up and liberally rouged, are dressed in splendid colourful costumes of embroidered brocade, and are decked with flags and elaborate headgear. The story is quite easy to follow as the drama unfolds and the heroes and villains make their exaggerated movements accompanied by live music. The stories are based on ancient Chinese epics dealing with love, treachery and war and inevitably end with the triumph of good over evil.

SPORTS AND RECREATION

For the sports lover, Singapore offers excellent facilities for all major sports. There are fifteen **golf courses** to choose from. All except Tanah Merah Country Club permit non-members to play, though weekends are usually reserved for members and most clubs require visitors to hold a handicap or proficiency certificate from a recognized club. A number of driving ranges are available for practice. Opening hours for golf clubs are normally 07:00 to 19:00; some offer night golfing until 23:00.

For **bowling**, contact the Singapore Tenpin Bowling Congress, 400 Balestier Road, #01-01 Balestier Plaza, Singapore 1232, tel 355 0136, fax 355 0390. Most bowling centres open at 09:00 and close about 01:00 or 02:00. Prices are higher after 18:00 and at weekends and public holidays.

For the watersports enthusiast there is **canoeing** at Changi Point, East Coast Park and Sentosa Island, as well as **scuba diving**, **windsurfing**, **sailing**, **water-skiing** and **swimming** (most big hotels in Singapore have swimming-pools). The Bishan Swimming Complex in Bishan Street is open to the public from 08:00 to 21:00.

Cycling is a favourite pastime for Singaporeans. Bicycles can be hired at the East Coast Bicycle Centre in East Coast Parkway (near the Food Centre), or at kiosks in Pasir Ris Park, Bishan Park and a number of others, as well as near the Pulau Ubin jetty point and at Sentosa Island Bicycle Station (near the ferry terminal).

The Singapore Sports Council exists to promote sports and physical fitness by planning, developing and maintaining public sports facilities. For further information on sports and recreation contact the Council at the National Stadium, Kallang, Singapore 1439, tel 345 7111, fax 340 9573.

> ### SPECTATOR SPORTS
>
> For those who would rather watch than play, details of sporting fixtures can be found in the daily press. The Singapore Cricket Club holds cricket matches on the Padang at weekends between March and October. Rugby is played here for the rest of the year. There are race meetings all year round at the Bukit Turf Club (see p 97) and regular polo matches from February to October at the Singapore Polo Club in Mount Pleasant Road. Football is played at the National Stadium: Singapore takes part in the Malaysian Cup. The Formula One Powerboat Grand Prix is held in Marina Bay in November.

Fifteen golf courses and a number of driving ranges cater for the many keen golfers in Singapore – both locals and visitors.

2
Downtown Singapore

What Singapore lacks in size, it makes up in innovation, creativity and surprises. Sightseeing in this city of contrasts is an assault on all the senses. You can either opt for leisurely sightseeing from the comfort of an air-conditioned bus with a guide as part of a conducted tour, or work out a do-it-yourself tour. Armed with a sense of adventure, the curiosity of a cat and a good city map, you cannot fail to enjoy this exciting place. Make full use of the public transport system: both the MRT and the bus services are efficient and cheap. Taxis are reasonably priced and are readily available (except in rush hours and when it is raining).

THE COLONIAL DISTRICT

It is only logical to follow in the footsteps of Raffles, and begin your exploration of the colonial district by starting at **Raffles' Landing Site** on North Boat Quay. The site is marked by a white marble replica of the statue of the founder himself, standing guard over a widened stretch of the Singapore River known as 'the belly of the carp'. There are several historical buildings and interesting landmarks in this area.

The Empress Place Museum **

Situated just to the right of the landing site at Empress Place, this neo-classical building was constructed in 1854 as a courthouse. It was later extended to house government offices. Today, the restored building is a museum and exhibition centre displaying archaeological treasures

MALAYSIA

SINGAPORE

Singapore City

DON'T MISS

*** The **Colonial District** with its many handsome edifices of a by-gone era.
** The 'Forbidden Hill' of **Fort Canning** with its beautiful garden and ancient tombs of Malay rulers.
*** The exquisite artefacts and works of art in the **National Museum**.
*** A Singapore Sling or afternoon tiffin in the elegant **Raffles Hotel**.
** The local colour (and maybe cricket) on the green expanse of the **Padang**.

Opposite: *The statue of the mythical Merlion stands guard at the mouth of the Singapore River.*

from China and other ancient civilizations. There are shops selling silk and handicrafts and a restaurant on the ground floor overlooking the river. Allow at least two to three hours to see the exquisite exhibitions. The museum opens daily from 09:00 to 18:30.

The Victoria Memorial Hall, now a concert hall, with the bronze statue of Raffles that originally stood on the Padang.

The Victoria Memorial Hall and Theatre ★★

The left wing of this grand building was erected in 1862 as the local town hall, while the right wing was added in 1905 as a tribute to Queen Victoria and was designed in the

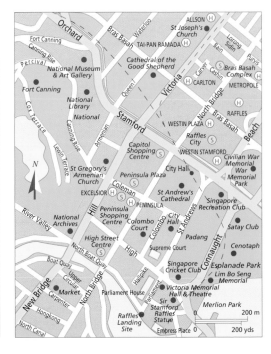

grandiose style of that era. The handsome façade with its columns and arches includes a tower containing a chiming clock donated by the Straits Trading Company in 1906. During the Japanese occupation this clock ran on Tokyo time, as did all the other clocks in the city at the command of the Imperial army. Today, this later section of the Hall is home to the Singapore Symphony Orchestra. **Raffles' Statue** stands in front of the building, with a plaque in tribute to the man 'to whose foresight and genius Singapore owes its existence and prosperity'. The bronze statue was unveiled in 1887, on the 50th anniversary of Queen Victoria's reign, and originally stood on the Padang. It was put away in storage by the Japanese forces during the occupation.

Cavenagh Bridge.

A BRIDGE TOO LOW

Cavenagh Bridge marks the beginning of the Colonial District. It was pre-fabricated in Scotland and erected in 1869 by Indian convict labourers to allay the inconvenience of crossing the Singapore River by boat. It was named after Major General Orfeur Cavenagh, Governor of the Straits Settlements from 1859-1867. The locals, however, complained that the bridge was too low to allow laden barges to pass under it at high tide. In the days of colonial arrogance, the official response was that the bridge was perfectly adequate and it was the river bed that needed dredging!

Parliament House **

Parliament House is one of the oldest government buildings in Singapore. Built in 1827 as a private mansion, it was later rented by the government and was eventually purchased in 1841, for use as a courthouse. It housed the Supreme Court until 1939, when the building was abandoned. It was extensively renovated in 1954 and was

SNOW ON THE PADANG

The Padang played an important part during the Japanese occupation from 1942-45. The Japanese would round people up there for interrogation and harangue them in public before marching them off for internment. The horror and hopelessness of the situation gave rise to the belief that Singapore would never be free until snow covered the Padang. It is said that a freak hailstorm blanketed the ground with ice one night and gave the people hope. Strange as this might sound in a tropical country, hailstorms had allegedly been recorded in Singapore in the past!

reopened as the Assembly House of the British colonial authority. Today it is the seat of parliament of the Republic. In front of it stands a bronze elephant, a gift in 1871 from King Chulalongkorn of Siam, who had been one of the charges of the English governess Anna of *The King and I* fame. Admission is by appointment only.

The Padang ★★

Across the road to the right is the green expanse of the Padang, the centre of colonial life for sporting events and social gatherings. It is still used for sport and for evening strolls by the local people. The **Singapore Cricket Club**, founded in 1852, sits at one end of the Padang, with the **Singapore Recreation Club** at the opposite end. Since the cricket club, the stronghold of British colonial society, admitted Europeans only, the recreation club was founded as the Eurasian community's answer to it. The cricket club remains accessible only to members and their guests, though its membership is now multiracial.

On St Andrew's Road beside the Padang is the **Supreme Court**, built in 1939 and one of the finest build-

Left: *The shining white Anglican cathedral of St Andrew's, built between 1856 and 1861 for the British colonialists.*

ings of the British era, with Corinthian columns, Italian murals and an imposing dome. Completed just before the Japanese invasion, the new building was adopted by the army of occupation as its headquarters. The **City Hall** stands next to it, on a site which witnessed the Japanese surrender in 1945 to Lord Louis Mountbatten, then Supreme Allied Commander of Southeast Asia. It now houses various government ministries. Visitors are allowed in the public gallery if correctly dressed – no shorts or slippers allowed – but two weeks' notice is required if you wish to see the rest of the interior.

Opposite: *The Singapore Cricket Club at one end of the Padang, the venue for most big sporting events in the city as well as National Day parades.*

St Andrew's Cathedral ★

The Cathedral, designed by Colonel Ronald MacPherson, was built using convict labour in 1862. It replaced an older church which had twice been hit by lightning. Worthy of note is the material used for the interior plaster: this is 'Madras chunam', a mixture of shell lime, egg white and sugar, mixed with water and coconut husk and polished to a rocky white gloss. Several services are held each day in various languages.

Below: *The Armenian Church of St Gregory the Illuminator in Hill Street.*

Armenian Church ★★

The oldest church in Singapore is the Armenian Church of St Gregory the Illuminator. Built in 1835, it was

THE FORBIDDEN HILL

Fort Canning has always been sacred to the Malays who referred to it as the 'Forbidden Hill'. It was believed to possess mysterious powers. During the occupation the Japanese raised their flag on the hill. The Malays felt this would augur badly for them and, surprisingly, when the occupying forces were told of this they respected the belief and removed the flag. The hill was also believed to have brought luck to Raffles, who built his home here.

The 'Garden City' of Singapore is full of green oases among its densely packed buildings.

designed by George Coleman and is considered his masterpiece. Its imposing white portico is supported by colonnades, flanked on both sides by elevated balustrades and crowned with a tall spire. Members of the Armenian community played an important part in the economic history of Singapore, notably the Sarkies brothers, who built **Raffles Hotel**, and Agnes Joachim, whose name was adopted for the national flower of Singapore, the purple-pink orchid, *Vanda* 'Miss Joachim', found growing in her garden in the 1890s. She is buried in the churchyard of St Gregory's.

Fort Canning ***

Strolling up Canning Rise from the Armenian Church, a flight of stairs will lead you to Fort Canning Park, where you will find memorials of early colonial pioneers and ancient royal Malay tombs. Here lies the **Keramat Iskandar Shah**, believed to be the tomb of the Sumatran prince who became the last king of Temasek, the old name for Singapore, in the 14th century. Raffles built his

first home here and it was generally believed that this sacred hill of the Malays had brought him the success he enjoyed. The fort itself, now in ruins, was built in 1859 to protect Singapore and to monitor shipping movement in the harbour. Burrowing through the hillside are the underground bunkers which housed the command post of the Allied forces during World War II. A 1km trail called the **19th Century Walk of History** enables visitors to retrace part of the history of that era.

The Christian cemetery here is the last resting-place of several famous colonial pioneers, such as the boat builder, Stephen Hallpike, architect George Coleman and the Armenian hotelier Aristakes Sarkies.

National Museum ★★★

This famous museum was built in 1887 and houses an amazing collection of Asian artefacts, in particular the **Haw Par Jade Collection**. You can also see examples of Peranakan culture, including fine furniture, porcelain and silverware. One of the museum's highlights is a three-dimensional reconstruction of the history of

Modern sculpture outside the National Museum in Stamford Road. The museum contains exhibits recording the history of Singapore as well as Malay, Chinese and Indian cultures.

BRAS BASAH ROAD

The name of this street, running from Dhoby Ghaut to Raffles Hotel, means 'wet rice' and is so named because of the wet rice traders who used to transport their produce by boat up the Stamford Canal and lay it out to dry on the banks.

A FLING WITH A SLING

A visit to Raffles Hotel is never complete without a glass of the famous Singapore Sling. For decades, visitors have flocked to sample this sweet sensation in the place where it was invented. Originally concocted as a 'ladies' drink', it is today enjoyed by both sexes. It was created in 1915 by Ngiam Tong Boon, a Hainanese bar captain at Raffles. The recipe for his unique cocktail, also known as the 'Million Dollar Cocktail', was a guarded secret then and visitors to the Raffles mini-museum can see the safe in which he locked it away. Today the recipe for the Sling is an open secret: 30ml gin; 7.5ml sweet vermouth; 120 ml pineapple juice; a dash of egg white and a dash of Angostura bitters. Serve in a tall cool glass...and the 'hint of paradise' is complete.

Singapore from sleepy sea town to thriving city. It is open from 09:00 to 17:00 (closed on Mondays). Allow 3 to 4 hours to see everything. Guided tours for small groups are available each morning from Tuesday to Friday.

Raffles Hotel ★★★

Affectionately known as 'The Grand Old Lady of the East', Raffles Hotel is redolent of old grandeur, timeless elegance and the celebrities who have been its guests. Founded in 1887 by the Armenian Sarkies brothers, proprietors of the Eastern and Oriental Hotel in Penang, it started as a humble 10-room hotel in an old bungalow at the corner of Beach and Bras Basah Roads. More wings were added over the next few years and Raffles' familiar main building, in elegant Renaissance style, dates from 1899, when it was the first building in Singapore to be equipped with electric light and the last word in opulence. The last tiger to be killed in Singapore was reportedly shot under the Bar and Billiard Room, then an elevated structure. Amongst the famous people who patronized and immortalized the hotel were Joseph Conrad, Rudyard Kipling, Somerset Maugham, Charlie Chaplin, Maurice Chevalier and Noel Coward. It was declared a national monument in 1987, then closed in 1989 for two years' restoration work. It re-opened in 1991, restored to its former glory, and continues to play host to the rich and famous.

Singapore's most famous landmark, the main building of Raffles Hotel, 'The Grand Old Lady of the East'.

Civilian War Memorial ★

Known affectionately by the locals as the 'Chopsticks' Memorial, and dedicated to the civilians who died during the Japanese occupation of World War II, this imposing white structure in its lovely setting of flowers and fountains tapers 70m (230ft) into the sky. The columns of four facets represent the four main ethnic groups of Singapore. Memorial Park is on Beach Road, a short walk from City Hall MRT.

Raffles City ★★

This massive complex on Bras Basah Road opposite Raffles Hotel houses two hotels, the Westin Plaza and the 73-storey Westin Stamford, as well as a convention centre and the Raffles City Shopping Complex. The Westin Stamford is the tallest hotel in the world, and the bar and restaurant located at the dizzy height of the top floor attract many sightseers eager to take in a bird's-eye view of the city.

Marina South City Park ★

This seafront park, south of the river and accessible from Marina Bay MRT, affords a splendid view of the sea. The breezy promenade features a huge sundial and a modern sculpture made of discs which revolve in the wind like a giant wind-chime. It is a popular venue for kite-flying while the calm waters are used for training by local rowing clubs and crews practising for the Dragon-Boat Race.

After a two-year restoration programme which sought to recreate the hotel's heyday in the 1920s, Raffles is once more the last word in luxury.

RIVAL HOTELS

'Feed at Raffles – where the food is excellent.' This ringing endorsement from the young Rudyard Kipling was enthusiastically taken up by Tigran Sarkies in the late 1880s. However, the article from which he extracted it was not so wholehearted in its praise: 'Providence conducted me along a beach, in full view of five miles of shipping – five solid miles of masts and funnels – to a place called Raffles Hotel, where the food is excellent as the rooms are bad. Let the traveller take note. Feed at Raffles and sleep at the Hotel de l'Europe.'

Work began on extensions to Raffles to improve the accommodation in 1890. The elegant Hotel de l'Europe was demolished to make way for the Supreme Court building in 1936.

THE WATERFRONT

The waterfront of Singapore has borne silent witness to
the trials and tribulations of a developing nation. When
Raffles landed in 1819, there was already some activity in
the small farming settlement of Malays and Chinese. It
was also infested with Bugis pirates who were said to
have littered the area with the dead bodies of their victims. A lesser man might have been deterred by this
macabre environment. Today, the only invaders are
tourists and the area is not even littered with rubbish,
but the bustling atmosphere remains – the place is full of
noise, people and colour. The old godowns and ware-

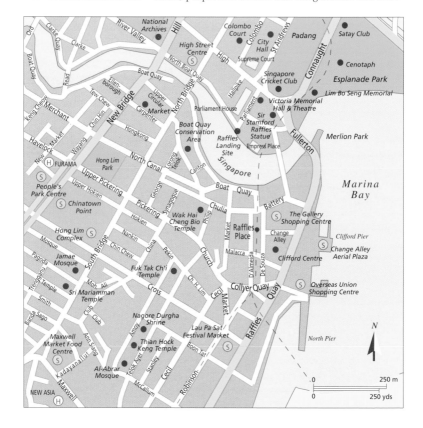

houses have been lovingly restored and converted into discos, bars, shops and restaurants, particularly along **Clarke** and **Boat Quays**. Bumboats still chug along the river ferrying passengers on joyrides and river cruises. Singapore has prospered but it has not quite forgotten its humble beginnings. It has restored the riverside to its former thriving state, albeit somewhat sanitized for the tourists.

Chinese lanterns illuminate the ornate tracery of Lau Pa Sat Festival Market. The filigree ironwork was cast in Glasgow and shipped out in 1894.

Waterside Attractions

Alight from Raffles Place MRT and stroll towards the waterfront through Change Alley, once a popular bazaar for bargain-hunting, to Collyer Quay. A pedestrian bridge, called **Change Alley Aerial Plaza**, a cleaned-up version of the once bustling bazaar full of money-changers and tailors, cuts across to **Clifford Pier**, from which Chinese junks and pleasure boats depart to take tourists on harbour cruises or trips to the southern islands (see page 101). To the south, towards the **business district** of Shenton Way and Robinson Road, is the **Lau Pa Sat Festival Market** (formerly Telok Ayer Market) in Boon Tat Street. Built in 1894, this ornate building is the last remaining Victorian filigree cast-iron structure in Southeast Asia. It was once a wet market and a food centre. It was dismantled during the building of the MRT and has been restored and converted into a festival market with shops, live entertainment and food

> ### CRUISING DOWN THE RIVER
>
> Don't miss seeing the city from the deck of a boat. A bumboat trip along the Singapore River offers a reminder of former days when these small wooden boats carried cargo rather than tourists. Old godowns and shophouses which have been restored and transformed into shops and restaurants (notably at Clarke Quay and Boat Quay) set the scene on the waterfront. The trips pass landmarks such as Raffles' Landing Site, Parliament House and the Merlion Statue. River cruises depart from Parliament Steps, Clifford Pier and Liang Court.

In the Boat Quay Conservation Area the river bank, once crowded with cargo boats and hawker stalls, is now lined with tables set out in front of the bars and restaurants in the converted shophouses.

centres serving local fare. In the evening, Boon Tat Street is closed to traffic and taken over by alfresco eating places. The market is open from 07:00 to 00:00.

A walk heading north up Fullerton Road will bring you to **Merlion Park** and the water-spouting statue of the **Merlion**, a mythical beast with the head of a lion and the body of a fish. Created in 1972 and installed at the mouth of the Singapore River, it has become the symbol of tourism and the national emblem. The **Queen Elizabeth Walk** across the Anderson Bridge is a park skirting the Padang and affording a scenic view of the sea. The pagoda-like **Lim Bo Seng Memorial** and the **Cenotaph** stand here, just before **Esplanade Park**, a popular place with the locals who frequent the **Satay Club** food centre at the northern end of the park.

Boat Quay ★★★

Situated opposite Raffles' Landing Site on the southern bank of the Singapore River is the Boat Quay Conservation Area. The once busy cargo loading bays have been transformed into a tourist attraction. Shophouses, warehouses and godowns have been spruced up and converted into restaurants, bars and entertainment centres. Bumboats which once carried cargo now transport tourists on river cruises. It is worthwhile joining one of these (best at high tide) to enjoy the views of riverside Singapore set against the gleaming skyscrapers in the background.

A HERO OF THE RESISTANCE

Colonel Lim Bo Seng was a wealthy and respected Straits-born Chinese, and was a member of the resistance movement Force 136. Betrayed by Lai Teck, the Secretary-General of the Malayan Communist Party and a traitor and double agent for the British, French and Japanese authorities, Lim Bo Seng was led to his capture by the Japanese in Perak. He was taken to Batu Gajah Prison where he was tortured to death for refusing to betray his comrades. After the war, his remains were located and returned to Singapore where a ceremony in his honour was held on the Padang. Escorted by armoured cars and guards of honour of British and Chinese troops from Force 136, his body was taken for burial in a grave on a hillside overlooking MacRitchie Reservoir.

Clarke Quay ★★★

Upstream from Boat Quay, this too is an area of restored warehouses and shophouses. It is a very lively place with a carnival atmosphere, clustered with market stalls set up on push carts, a wide choice of restaurants, bars and open-air eating places, and a Disney-style adventure ride. Clowns on stilts and wayside portrait artists entertain the passers-by.

The Quay is divided into five areas: Merchants' Court, the Cannery, Shophouse Row, Traders' Market and the Foundry. Traditional *tongkangs*, or junks, are moored along the bank, serving drinks and snacks. In the cool evening breeze by the river you can try the 'steamboat' at the alfresco self-service restaurant called the **Raffles Company**. In spite of its marine connotations, the steamboat has nothing to do with sailing but is a steaming pot of soup, kept simmering over a burner, into which you dunk morsels of seafood or meat and vegetables, cooking them at your table. For a modest sum you can help yourself to as much food as you can possibly eat, complete with dessert.

As dusk falls, a vibrant, carnival atmosphere prevails along Clarke Quay.

RIVER VALLEY

River Valley Road runs parallel with the Singapore River along its northern bank, commencing at Coleman Bridge. This is an old residential area of quaint houses inhabited by a mixed community. A banner of mango leaves with an icon of a Hindu deity suspended above the front door will indicate that a house belongs to an Indian family, while a mirror strategically placed over the door to evade evil spirits indicates that a Chinese family is in residence. The area has a church, a Hindu temple, a synagogue and a Chinese temple. The narrow streets are flanked by antiques emporia and craft shops where you can watch the craftsmen at work making camphorwood-lined teak chests of intricate oriental design or Art Deco models to order. Jewellery lovers will want to hunt out the shop selling loose beads and pendants fashioned from semi-precious stones, carved cinnabar and wood, coral and jade which will be strung according to your own design. If you have time to wander at leisure, this area is worth wearing your shoes out for.

Fort Canning Aquarium *

This aquarium in River Valley Road, formerly called the Van Cleef Aquarium, houses 500 species of tropical and temperate aquatic and marine creatures, including sharks, the flamboyant lion fish and crocodiles. Corals and other marine life forms are also displayed. It is open from 09:00 to 21:30 daily; feeding time is at 12:00.

Sri Thandayuthapani Temple **

Located just north of River Valley Road on Tank Road, this temple is also known as the **Hindu Chettiars' Temple**. It was financed by the Chettiars, wealthy money-lenders from the Madras region who were encouraged to settle in Singapore by the British. The temple was constructed in the 1980s on a site originally occupied by an older building of 1859. Its notable features are its 48 engraved glass pañels depicting various deities, set into the roof at angles designed to catch the rays of the rising and setting sun. The temple has many magnificent statues and shrines dedicated to members of the Hindu pantheon, including the 120cm (4ft) peacock statue with a solid gold cobra coiled around it. Besides being the

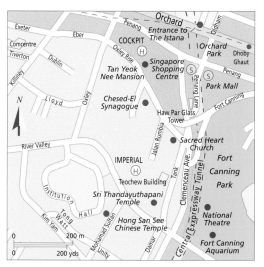

Opposite: *The gilded gopuram, or entrance tower, of the Sri Thandayuthapani Temple. The temple is dedicated to Lord Subramaniam whose birthday is celebrated by the festival of Thaipusam.*

TAN KAH KEE

An outstanding member of Singapore's Chinese community was the philanthropist Tan Kah Kee. Born near Amoy in China in 1873, he came to Singapore, penniless, at the age of 17 to work in a rice shop. By 1904 he had set up his own rice shop and pineapple processing factory, and later diversified into rubber, rice milling and shipping. By World War I his company was the most prominent in Singapore with holdings in Malaya, Siam and China. Having experienced hardship himself, he donated much of his wealth to the building of primary schools and financed a major part of Amoy University. He founded the first Chinese middle school in Singapore in 1919, educating boys up to pre-university level. He set up a Chinese newspaper, Nanyang Siang Pau, and devoted most of his later years to Chinese patriotic movements. He died in 1961 in the Chinese village in which he was born.

ultimate destination of the annual Thaipusam procession (see page 26), it is also the focal point for the celebration of the Navarathiri festival. In honour of the goddesses Dhurga, Lakshmi and Saraswathi, classical Indian music and dance are performed here over nine nights each October.

Further up Tank Road is the **Sacred Heart Church**, whose pillared interior walls and peculiar corners have given rise to the suspicion that it was built inside out in error. Nearby is the striking **Teochew Building**, clan house of the prosperous Teochew clan, built in the style of a Chinese palace with its pagoda-like green roof. The **Tan Yeok Nee Mansion** in Clemenceau Avenue was

The Church of the Sacred Heart in Tank Road. A legend that it was built inside out has grown up because of the style of its interior walls.

The Teochew Building, the palatial clan house of this commercially dominant Chinese clan.

built for a member of this clan in 1885, in a Chinese style unusual for the period when most building in Singapore echoed European designs. Badly damaged during the Japanese occupation, it was restored by the Salvation Army, whose headquarters it became. Near it is the **Chesed-El Synagogue**, built in 1905 by the wealthy Jewish businessman, Menasshah Meyer, whose family still maintain it as a place of worship.

Hong San See Chinese Temple ★★

At 31 Mohammed Sultan Road, to the south of River Valley Road, you will encounter the Hong San See Temple. Now gazetted as a national monument, it was built by Fukien immigrants in 1829 in Tras Street, and moved to its present site in 1907. The temple is sited facing water and backed by a hill, and is therefore believed to have very good *feng shui. Feng shui*, literally the science of wind and water, is central to the art of geomancy. It studies the harmony of cosmic elements on the sites of buildings, with the aim of attracting good luck and dispelling bad. It continues to be an important factor in the siting, size and design of Chinese buildings and their furnishings. The Hong San See Temple is dedicated to the god of filial piety, a duty which is of paramount importance in Chinese society. It is said that the deity sold himself into slavery to pay for the upkeep of his parents' graves.

NUTMEG TREES

You would be hard pressed to find a nutmeg tree in Singapore today but the island was once covered with them. Nutmeg plantations used to clad the area around Orchard Road, Scotts Road and Mount Elizabeth. Captain William Scott, the son of the British explorer James Scott, was a nutmeg and cocoa plantation owner here and Scotts Road was named after him. Four million nuts were produced in 1848, but soon afterwards the plantations were devastated by pests and most dwindled into small plots as the land was sold off to property developers. Today, when towering skyscrapers, shopping malls and offices line these streets, it is hard to imagine that the area was once infested with tigers and that wealthy merchants with their retinues of servants used to stroll here in the cool shade of the nutmeg trees.

ORCHARD ROAD

This is the main shopping thoroughfare of Singapore, lined from end to end with swanky malls, punctuated with luxury hotels and office buildings rising to intoxicating heights. The pavement is a seething mass of jostling shoppers and tourists, whilst the road teems with traffic. From November right through to the New Year every year, Orchard Road is an extravaganza of Christmas lights and decorations so grand and brilliant that it makes Disneyworld look drab.

Peranakan Showhouse Museum ★★★

Orchard Road is essentially one big shopping centre, but midway along this busy street is **Peranakan Place** where six old shophouses have been restored to their former glory with decorative tiles and fretwork painted in pastel colours. The Museum, at 180 Orchard Road, depicts the affluent lifestyle of the Peranakans, or Straits Chinese, the descendants of early Chinese settlers who married the native Malays in the 15th and 16th centuries. Unlike

The futuristic outline of a new shopping plaza along Orchard Road.

Spicy Nonya food is served in the restaurant in Peranakan Place, near the Peranakan Showhouse Museum.

the later Chinese immigrants of the 19th century, the Peranakans embraced and assimilated aspects of Malay culture into their Chinese lifestyle. With their astute business sense, many Straits Chinese families accumulated large fortunes, and their homes were lavishly and tastefully furnished: the exquisite furniture, colourful Chinese porcelain known as Nonyaware, intricate beaded embroidery and beautiful ornaments shown in the museum are fine examples of the heirlooms of this unique culture. You can sample their renowned spicy cuisine in an open-air restaurant in Peranakan Place. The museum is open from 10:30 to 15:30, Monday to Friday.

Cuppage Terrace and Emerald Hill ★★
Set just off Orchard Road are the colourful pink-tinted buildings of Cuppage Terrace, with its shopping centres and plazas. Running along the left-hand side of the Cuppage building is **Emerald Hill Road**, one of Singapore's most charismatic residential areas. Here, charming old-fashioned houses, mostly built in the 1920s, have been carefully renovated as part of an official conservation project. Their ornate façades reflect both European and Asian architectural styles: Doric and Corinthian columns frame French louvred windows, whilst *pintu pagar*, or fence doors, guard the front entrances. These decoratively carved fence doors also serve a practical purpose, allowing fresh air into the house whilst preserving the privacy of the occupants.

SHOPPING

Singapore has long been acknowledged as a wonderful place to shop and indeed travellers from all over the world make a point of stopping over in the city to snap up a bargain or two. It is also a favourite pastime for the local populace to browse in the endless array of shopping complexes and department stores. The air-conditioning and the state-of-the-art window displays are added attractions for both locals and visitors. Although prices are not as competitive as they once were, the sheer breadth of choice means there are still bargains to be had.

NGEE ANN CITY

Reputedly the largest shopping centre in South-east Asia, Ngee Ann City's striking architecture is a dominating landmark in Orchard Road. Its six floors are packed with a vast range of merchandise and include high fashion boutiques and Tiffany's. Its anchor tenant, **Takashimaya Shopping Centre**, features a department store, cultural facilities, specialist shops, restaurants, a health club, a swimming-pool and function halls.

Opposite: *The main building of the Goodwood Park Hotel, built in 1900 as the clubhouse of the German Teutonia Club.*

Goodwood Park Hotel *

The Goodwood Park Hotel along Scotts Road is a distinguished national landmark. It started life in 1900 as the Teutonia Club for the German community in Singapore, and was designed by the Singapore firm of Swan and Maclaren in the style of a Rhine castle to reflect its German heritage, with a central tower as its showpiece.

The first Germans to arrive in Singapore came as entrepreneurs in the 1850s, prospecting for investments and seeking employment. In common with the rest of the European community, they settled around Orchard, Scotts and Tanglin Roads. They formed the Teutonia Club in 1856 and the first clubhouse was built in 1861, but as the membership grew a much grander building was commissioned on the same site. The building cost S$20,000 and its grand opening was the social event of the decade. The Teutonia Club became the toast of the town and was patronized by the rich and famous. It was a popular venue for grand social occasions and classical concerts.

During World War I the club was seized as enemy property and was auctioned off in 1918 to the Manassehs, a wealthy Jewish family. It was renamed Goodwood Hall after Goodwood House in England and Mrs Ezekiel

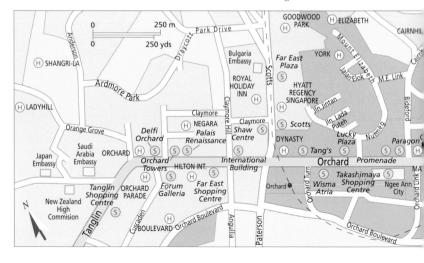

Manasseh's family home. It was restored and opened as a restaurant-cum-entertainment venue in 1922, when one of the year's highlights there was a performance by the world-famous ballerina Anna Pavlova. It was turned into a hotel in 1929, catering for businessmen from Malaya, and became one of the best hotels in Singapore by the end of the 1930s, counting the Duke of Windsor amongst its distinguished guests. Today, Goodwood Park remains a hotel of distinction, and the imposing tower of the main building was gazetted as a national monument in 1989.

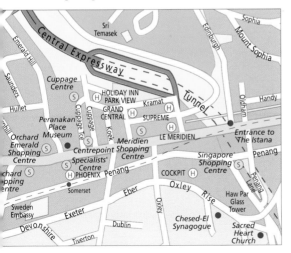

WHERE TO SHOP

Orchard Road is the main shopping district of Singapore where department stores and shops line each side of the street from end to end. Notable stores are: **CK Tang**: five floors of shops selling goods from household to fashion and electronic products; **Centrepoint**: a wide variety of consumer goods including fashions, toys, furniture, stationery, sports goods and books; **Far East Plaza**, **Far East Shopping Centre**, **Lucky Plaza**: popular with the locals for bargain-hunting; **Midpoint**: music and art a speciality; **OG Building**: clothes; **Orchard Plaza** and **Orchard Towers**: a wide choice of electronic goods and cameras; the **Promenade**, **Shaw Centre**, **Shaw House (Isetan)** and **Specialist Shopping Centre**: fashion, jewellery, shoes and accessories; **Paragon**, **Palais Renaissance**, **Liat Towers** and **Tudor Court**: mostly designer clothes from the West and some local couturiers.

TANGLIN SHOPPING CENTRE

For antiques and exquisite oriental treasures, this is the place. Antique maps and prints are specialities here in addition to intricately woven oriental carpets. **China Silk House** and **Design Thai** are amongst its tenants selling souvenirs, arts and crafts.

TAKING IT WITH YOU

In a materialistic world, even the dead are indulged with luxuries. Often a medium is consulted first to find out what the deceased might want. For those who enjoyed a good life on earth, their families will buy effigies of Mercedes or BMWs, American Express cards, servants, a house and a television (and possibly nowadays a mobile phone and a fax machine). If the deceased was single, a spouse effigy will also be included. These earthly gifts, together with paper 'hell' money, will be burnt at the funeral in the belief that they will be despatched with the dead to the next world.

A fine example of the effigy-maker's skill: a paper motorbike to be burnt at a Chinese funeral.

THE ETHNIC QUARTERS

Beneath the veneer of affluent sophistication can still be found a very different Singapore, steeped in tradition, culture and superstition. When the major pioneer migratory groups of Chinese, Indians and Arabs began to flock into the country in its early days, they were each designated their own neighbourhood by Sir Stamford Raffles. The distinctive characteristics of these areas still survive: the heritage of 'endangered Singapore' is kept alive by the individual ethnic groups. In recent years the government has made a concerted effort to preserve and restore many beautiful old buildings and shophouses, the remaining legacy of the city's rich and colourful past.

CHINATOWN

South of the Singapore River and overshadowed by the soaring modern office blocks of the financial district lie the shuttered shophouses of this traditionally Chinese domain. The kaleidoscopic feast of colour is the first thing that will hit any visitor. The flamboyance of the many temples, and the rainbow hues of all manner of goods, clustered in the shops and spilling over into the five-foot way, will mesmerize you. As you wander through this timeless place the pungent smell of traditional Chinese medicine will assault your nostrils at the same time as the tantalizing aromas from the many coffee shops selling mouth-watering delicacies and steaming noodles. Watch out for the famous sweet barbecued pork being grilled over red-hot charcoal along the five-foot way. This speciality is in great demand during Chinese New Year, to be given as a present or served to guests.

In the old days, the early Chinese settlers used to live in squalid, cramped conditions where it was not uncommon for many people to share one room, some sleeping under the beds of other families. Today, Chinatown has been cleaned up and restored, somehow robbing it of some of its authenticity. The alleyways and narrow streets, however, have stood firm against modernity. A traditional way of life still prevails among the older generation. Stroll through Club Street and Ann Siang Road, a Hokkien stronghold in the 1870s, to see songbirds tweeting away in their gilded cages while the 'informal national flag of Singapore' –

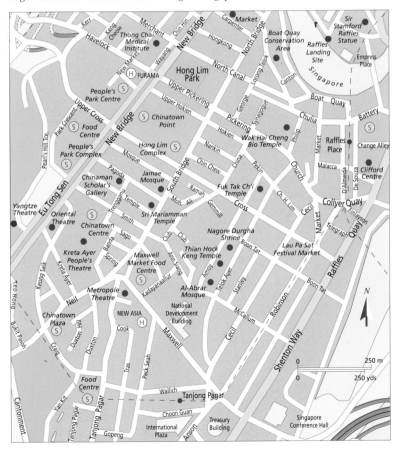

Right: *Songbirds are brought out on Sunday mornings to show off their prowess. Hanging the birds up high is considered to improve their songs.*
Opposite: *The Thian Hock Kheng Temple, the city's oldest Chinese temple, built by Hokkien immigrants grateful for a safe voyage.*

FEATHERED SONGSTERS

The ancient Chinese pastime of keeping songbirds is thriving in Singapore. Early Sunday mornings are especially devoted to assemblies of proud owners at coffee shops or pre-arranged venues in Tiong Bahru on the outskirts of Chinatown, Jalan Besar or Petain Road in Little India. The pampered pets are kept in beautiful gilded or cane cages, with pretty shade covers and porcelain feeding dishes containing live crickets, which are said to improve the birds' voices. The birds are grouped according to their breed and warble together, some melodiously while others need further singing lessons. Some owners encourage their birds to sing by playing recorded melodies by prize-winning songbirds in the hope that they will pick up a few tips. Talented songsters can fetch high prices, while those who are tonedeaf and prove unable to learn to sing well are sometimes released into the wild.

washing draped over long bamboo poles – flutters listlessly in the soft breeze. A bean curd and noodle restaurant along the street serves tasty snacks. A discreet peer into some of the shophouses through old-fashioned wooden bars across the door will reveal ancestral altars and joss-sticks burning, sometimes with offerings of oranges. Up Ann Siang Hill, craftsmen are busy making gaudy lion and dragon heads for dance troupes out of canes and coloured paper, complete with moving eyebrows and eyelids for effect, distinguishing between a northern lion which has more hair than its southern cousin with short hair in the warmer clime of South China.

Many craftsmen continue to ply their age-old trades in these crowded streets. There is the clog maker, knocking into shape the traditional wooden footwear (especially useful for shopping in the wet market, as it elevates your feet from the drenched floor). For the tea connoisseur there are quaint little tea shops that raise tea-making into an art form and offer a vast choice of tea and utensils. The ancient art of calligraphy is still evident, while effigy and joss-stick makers are kept busy by the continuing demand for traditional Chinese funeral rites. Shops in Temple Street and Sago Street make cane and coloured paper effigies of houses, cars, money and other necessaries, which are burnt to journey with the deceased into the next world. Sago Street became a kind of hospice for the Chinese. Dying elderly relatives used to be sent to nursing homes here to await death, as the Chinese consider it bad luck to have a death at home.

Singapore River
Sri Mariamman Temple
Marina Bay
Thian Hock Kheng Temple

Chinaman Scholar's Gallery *

In the midst of Chinatown at 14B Trengganu Street near the Sri Mariamman Temple, is a recreation of the home of a Chinese scholar of the 1920s and 30s. The style of the period is faithfully reconstructed in the kitchen, bedroom, dining and living areas filled with furniture, porcelain, traditional clothes, musical instruments and photographs depicting the lives of the pioneer Chinese settlers. The gallery is open from 09:00 to 16:00 (closed on Sundays and public holidays).

Thian Hock Kheng Temple **

The 'Temple of Heavenly Happiness' in Telok Ayer Street was built in 1841 and is dedicated to Ma Chor Por, the Protector of Sailors. The site was originally on the waterfront, before land reclamation shifted the harbour to the east, and in the early days Hokkien immigrants used to gather here as they came ashore to give thanks for a safe journey. The deity's statue was brought over from China in 1840 and was paraded through the streets with much aplomb. A pair of stone lions guards the entrance to the temple: make sure you

TURF LUCK

Next to the effigy of Tua Pek Kong in the Fuk Tak Ch'i Temple is the statue of a horse with its legs bound. This practice dates back to the days when Hakka women used to tie the legs of horse statues in the temple to ensure the safe return of their menfolk when they left their village for faraway places to search for work. Nowadays, avid backers of racehorses pray to this horse and often untie the bindings on its legs to enable it to go faster!

Right: *The entrance to the Tamil Muslim Nagore Durgha Shrine.*
Opposite: *A fortune-teller with her attendant parrot.*

TREASURES OF THE SEA

Many shops in Chinatown specialize in Chinese herbs, medicines and delicacies. **Shark's fin** is the premier delicacy in Chinese cuisine. It has no taste of its own but its crunchy and rubbery texture and golden hue is greatly enhanced by a gentle simmer in chicken stock flavoured with crab meat, shredded chicken and eggs and cooked to a delicious thick soup.

The **abalone** reigns supreme in Chinese seafood cuisine and commands a high price, dried or fresh. It is usually cooked in soup, stir-fried lightly with vegetables or eaten on its own as it has a naturally rich flavour.

The **sea cucumber**, resembling a giant sea slug, has a slimy rubbery texture and is usually cooked with vegetables in soup or braised with Chinese mushrooms.

The treasures of the sea attain their ultimate grandeur in an exquisite, not to mention expensive, dish called Buddha Jumps Over the Wall, an extravagant broth of abalone, highest quality sharks' fin, scallops, fish maw, sea cucumber and Chinese mushrooms, fit for an emperor.

twirl the stone ball in the mouth of the lion for good luck as you step over the high door sill which is built in this way to prevent evil spirits from entering. The fabric of the temple is very international: Dutch Delft tiles line the courtyard, English motif tiles decorate the altar and Scottish cast iron girdles the doorway, supported by granite pillars entwined with dragons. The inner altar is dedicated to Kuan Yin, the Goddess of Mercy, while smaller shrines are devoted to various deities, including one featuring statues of horses where devotees pray for good fortune at the races. This is the oldest Chinese temple in Singapore and has been designated a national monument.

Just to the left of the temple is another national monument, the **Nagore Durgha Shrine**. It was built by Tamil Muslims in 1830 in a unique blend of classical and southern Indian Muslim motifs, surmounted by turrets. To the right of the Chinese temple is the **Al Abrar Mosque**, a restored 19th-century building with a carpeted and tiled courtyard and an arch, the Mehrab, indicating the direction of Mecca.

Fuk Tak Ch'i Temple *

The Fuk Tak Ch'i Temple (the Temple of Prosperity and Virtue) in Telok Ayer Street is one of the oldest buildings in Singapore. Constructed in 1820, it was rebuilt in 1825 as a Shentoist temple: a combination of Buddhism, Confucianism and Taoism. Here spiritual contacts with the dead can be channelled through the temple mediums. This Hakka temple is dedicated to Tua Pek Kong, the God of Wealth, whose statue is arrayed in sackcloth and his lips smeared with opium.

Sri Mariamman Temple ***

Along South Bridge Road is the oldest and largest Hindu temple in the country, built in 1843. It replaced an earlier structure on this site erected in 1827 by Narian Pillai, who had arrived in Singapore on Raffles' own ship. The magnificent pagoda-like entrance-tower, or *gopuram*, restored in 1984, is bedecked with carvings of numerous deities from the Hindu pantheon. Bells and banana fronds frame its doorway and colourful frescoes span the ceiling. The annual fire-walking festival of **Thimithi** is celebrated here around November, when devotees walk barefoot across a bed of red-hot embers.

Tanjong Pagar Conservation Area **

Lying just south of Chinatown between Tanjong Pagar Road and Neil Road, this is an interesting area to explore with its attractive Peranakan shophouses which are the subject of an extensive restoration programme. The pastel-painted terraces offer an array of eating-places, night-spots, souvenir shops and art galleries.

FORTUNE-TELLING

In spite of their thoroughly modern glossy image, Singaporeans still seek the advice of fortune-tellers to guide them in their future. A businessman would not dream of building an office block or a house without first consulting the *feng shui* expert, the geomancer, to seek out a favourable site and auspicious position for the building. Women can be observed at temples casting kidney-shaped wooden blocks, called *mu bei*, to the ground: the way the blocks fall indicates an answer from the gods. Spiritual advice can also be sought from shaking bamboo fortune-telling sticks from a container until one falls out. The inscriptions on the sticks are usually interpreted by a resident temple attendant. Along Serangoon Road, fortunes are told through cards picked at random by parrots, from which the fortune-teller will spin a tale of your future.

Baskets of every size and shape spill onto the pavement of a shop in Arab Street.

ARAB STREET

Amongst the first traders to arrive in Singapore were the Arabs, dealing in gold, coffee, spices and pearls. Today, the area around Arab Street retains its distinctive flavour and Aladdin's cave atmosphere. The numerous shops are a riot of colour, overflowing with shimmering silks, batik and other textiles, all at bargain prices. Baskets, some quite big enough to hide one of Ali Baba's forty thieves, festoon the shopfronts, while the five-foot way is filled with goods from antiques, trinkets and leather goods to Turkish scents. Don't miss the *roti prata* restaurants, where the making of these wheat pancakes is a dramatic spectacle. The *prata* man, with nimble fingers and great panache, will flatten, tease and twirl the dough in the air until it is paper thin. It is then flicked onto a hot griddle and within minutes is ready to be dunked into spicy curry sauce or sprinkled with sugar, as the fancy takes you.

The noise of the street vendors, punctuated by the regular wailing of the *muezzin* calling the faithful to prayer, seems a world away from the thoroughly modern business district of Singapore.

THE ART OF BATIK-MAKING

The batik sold in Arab Street is imported from Indonesia or Malaysia. Batik is usually made from cotton or silk. Traditional motifs include flowers and stylized animals, which are created by the application of wax to the required design, dyeing, drying and repeating the process with different coloured dyes until the pattern is complete over the whole length of fabric. It is a lengthy and laborious process and takes many hours of patience and deft hands. The end results are used for clothing, wall hangings, scarves, sarongs, handbags, tablecloths, place-mats and other accessories. Batik and silk are good buys in Arab Street where shoppers can haggle with the textile merchants for the best price.

Sultan Mosque ★★★

Arab Street is dominated by the Sultan Mosque, the focal point of Islamic Singapore. Built in 1928 to a design by the colonial firm of Swan and Maclaren, who were also the architects for the Victoria Memorial Hall, it replaced the original 1820s mosque on this site. Its massive golden dome and huge prayer hall make it one of Singapore's most imposing religious buildings. During Ramadan the streets around the mosque take on a carnival atmosphere as hundreds of stalls sell delicacies with which Muslims break their fast each dusk.

Istana Kampong Glam **

East of the mosque, at Sultan Gate, is the old royal Muslim quarter, in which stands the mansion of Sultan Hussein Mohammed Shah of Singapore. Built in 1840, it has seen better days, although it manages to cling to some of its old grandeur. The house next door to it was another royal home, once owned by the half-brother of Sultan Hussein's grandson, Tengku Allum.

The beautiful Sultan Mosque, the principal place of worship for Singapore's Muslim population.

Hajjah Fatimah Mosque **

Slightly further away from Arab Street proper is this tranquil mosque in Beach Road. It was built in 1846 by its namesake, a Melakan-born Malay who married a wealthy Bugis merchant. She amassed a fortune after her husband's death from her astute management of his shipping business, and built the mosque, to a British-influenced design, in the grounds of her home after she had moved away from the area, tired of being constantly robbed. Arab Street in those days was a favourite haunt of thieves who preyed on its rich residents. Hajjah Fatimah's tomb, together with that of her daughter Raja Sitti and her son-in-law Syed Ahmad Alsagoff, lies in the grounds of the mosque which today is taken care of by the Alsagoff family.

Bugis Street **

Bugis Street was once the most interesting place to visit in Singapore for a taste of the local colour and vibrant nightlife. It was the haunt of transvestites, frolicking amongst the tourists and sailors who flocked to the sleazy street every night for entertainment and a voyeuristic thrill. The drag queens in their splendid, often revealing, attire would prance up and down the street in their stilettos, posing for pictures with willing

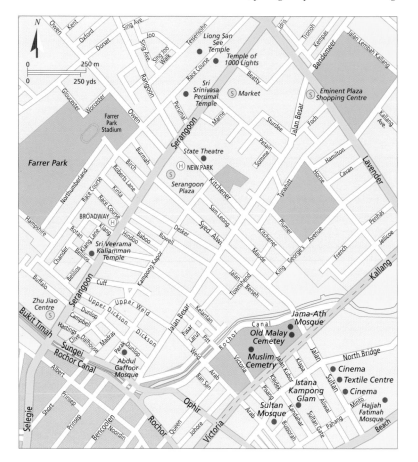

Eating out in New Bugis Street, a pale imitation of the old centre of Singapore's nightlife which was demolished to make way for the MRT.

THE JEWELS OF LITTLE INDIA

Gold and silver jewellery have always played an important part in Indian culture, not just as a measurement of wealth or as dowries for women, but also for religious purposes. The streets in Little India are thronged with shops displaying a dazzling array of jewels. Some sell silver sheets embossed with parts of the body, to be used as temple offerings when seeking a cure for a specific ailment. Silver amulets are worn for luck and protection from evil spirits, while fine silver spears are used to pierce the bodies of devotees in a Thaipusam procession. Heavy ropes of sovereign coins strung on ornate chains are popular for dowries. Encrusted earrings with long chains with hooks on each end are worn by Indian women with the chain hooked into the hair as a traditional dual-purpose accessory. Gold jewellery in Singapore is of 22 or 24 carat and is priced according to the weight of gold and the design of the piece. Current market prices for gold are usually displayed on a board in the shop; when a buyer selects a piece of jewellery, the goldsmith will weigh it and charge accordingly.

patrons for a fee and a drink. Good times were had by all! In 1985, Bugis Street was demolished when the MRT was built, and in a campaign to clean up Singapore's image, the transvestites with their frocks and high heels were sent packing, thus ending the 'pink era' of Singapore's favourite tourist attraction.

Today, **Bugis Village** in New Bugis Street is a sanitized recreation of the old street, minus the transvestites and the rowdy sailors. It is thronged with market stalls selling fake designer goods, clothes, souvenirs and fruits. There are food centres serving local fare and delicacies. An attempt has been made to reinstate the local colour but it lacks the ambience of the old street. However, it's still worth a visit if you want an evening out.

LITTLE INDIA

In essence, the district around Serangoon Road is the Indian sub-continent condensed and transported to Singapore. Originally a swamp, the siting of brick kilns and lime-pits here by the colonial government in the 1820s led Indian labourers to settle in the district, and they made it their own.

Little India features all aspects of Indian culture and customs. The aroma of spices and jasmine hangs in the

THE MONK AND THE OCTOPUS

Legend has it that a monk set out from China to collect the Tripitaka, the sacred canon of Theravada Buddhism, from Buddha in India, and enlisted the help of a passing tortoise to ferry him across a lake. The tortoise promised to help on condition that the monk asked Buddha to grant it longevity. The monk collected the holy script and asked the tortoise to help him again, but confessed that he had forgotten the tortoise's request. The tortoise, in anger, dived into the lake, leaving the monk to drown. He managed to struggle ashore and hastily spread the holy scroll out to dry. Exhausted, he fell asleep. Meanwhile, an octopus climbed ashore and licked up all the ink from the scroll. The monk tried in vain to get the octopus to reveal the secrets of the scripture by bashing it on the head. Today, while chanting the *sutras*, devotees symbolically hit a wooden octopus with a mallet to make it yield the secret of the Tripitaka. The legend also explains why the octopus has ink in its body.

air of the narrow streets, flanked by shophouses selling garlands of flowers strung by men with nimble fingers to decorate altars, adorn a woman's hair or a taxi driver's dashboard shrine. Some shops stock special Indian cosmetics: turmeric powder or cream for the complexion, henna to decorate the hands and feet, especially for weddings, perfumed oils for the skin and kohl pencils for the eyes. Others specialize in spices for Indian cuisine and there are communal mills to which housewives bring their fresh spice mixtures each day to be ground by the miller for a small fee. The tempting aroma of curry wafts from numerous restaurants and stalls sell colourful Indian sweetmeats.

The **Zhujiao Centre** in Buffalo Road is an interesting place to explore, with its large wet market, food centres and shops selling electronic equipment, clothes and bric-à-brac at bargain prices.

Veerama Kaliamman Temple *
The old Tamil proverb, 'Do not settle in a land without temples', prompted the community to build an abun-

A shopkeeper sits in one of Little India's five-foot ways.

dance of temples in the area. This one in Belilios Road was built in 1855 by indentured Bengali labourers. Its name means 'Kali the Courageous' and it is dedicated to the fierce goddess Kali whose jet-black statue adorns the altar. Lesser shrines are devoted to Ganesh, the elephant-headed god of wisdom and Murugah, the conqueror of evil.

A vivid piece of carving at the Veerama Kaliamman Temple.

Srinivasa Perumal Kovil Temple ★★

Situated in Serangoon Road, this temple, a national monument, is the starting-point of the annual Thaipusam procession (see page 26). It was built on the site of a pond used for ritual washing which was purchased for S$5 in 1855. The temple is built in honour of Perumal, also known as Vishnu, 'the admirable one', who is believed to have been reincarnated nine times to save mankind. His nine manifestations are depicted on the tiers of the towering *gopuram* at the entrance. Inside are shrines to the god himself, his two wives, Lakshmi and Andal, and his mythical bird, the Garuda.

Temple of 1000 Lights ★★

This simple temple in Race Course Road is also called the Sakaya Muni Buddha Gaya Temple. Its focal point is a 15m (50ft) seated Buddha surrounded by a huge number of light bulbs. Frescoes depicting the life of Buddha are etched at the base of the giant statue. Don't miss the secret reclining Buddha hidden in an underground alcove accessed by a short flight of stairs at the back of the shrine beneath the seated Buddha.

Abdul Gaffoor Mosque ★

Tucked away on Dunlop Street, this mosque was built in 1910 to replace a more modest building. It is designed in a Moorish style with a peaceful courtyard. To the left of the prayer hall by the washing area hangs a framed genealogical tree which traces the common lineage of Christians and Muslims. Biblical figures such as Jesus, Abraham, Noah, Jacob and Joseph can be found listed by their Arabic names.

LITTLE INDIA'S STREET NAMES

Many of the area's streets bear names of colonial politicians or army personnel who served in India. Hastings Road, for instance, is named after Warren Hastings, the first governor-general of Bengal, Clive Street after Robert Clive, Baron of Plassey, who consolidated British control of India in 1757, and Campbell Lane after Sir Colin Campbell who suppressed the Indian mutiny and freed Lucknow in 1857.

Singapore City at a Glance

BEST TIMES TO VISIT

As Singapore is not affected by the monsoon season as such, any time of the year is a good time to visit. Nov–Jan are the wettest months, July is driest, while Feb is the sunniest. There are festivals and events throughout the year (see festival calendar on p 24) and the National Day celebration falls on 9 Aug.

GETTING THERE

Being one of the principal air hubs of the world, Singapore is served by 63 international airlines from 54 countries. Its flag carrier, Singapore Airlines, flies to more than 80 cities in 42 countries. It is one of the major ports of call for luxury cruise ships. It is also well served by the North-South Expressway from the Thai border through Malaysia and across the Straits of Johor via the causeway. In addition there are frequent daily bus and rail services to Peninsular Malaysia. Check with your travel agent for details.

GETTING AROUND

Travelling within Singapore is easy and inexpensive with its well-planned roads and public transport systems. Extensive bus networks complement the efficient MRT system, while taxis are plentiful. Trishaws provide a novel option for sightseeing around the city.

MRT (Mass Rapid Transport) This modern air-conditioned passenger electric train service covers 42 stations. There are three lines: the East-West line from Pasir Ris to Boon Lay; the North-South line from Yishun to Marina Bay; the line from Choa Chu Kang to Jurong East. Each route is colour-coded and directions are marked on the platforms; travel maps and guides are available at all stations. Trains operate at intervals of 3–8 mins from 06:00 to 00:00. There are ticket machines in the stations. TransitLink fare-cards (for which a deposit is charged) are available at most MRT stations and at bus interchanges. They are valid on the MRT as well as bus services operated by Singapore Bus Service (SBS) and the Trans Island Bus Service (TIBS). Any unused fares, plus the deposit, are refundable. A Tourist Souvenir ticket is also available from MRT stations in the city. Contact TransitLink hotline 776 0100.

Buses
SBS and TIBS bus services operate regular and inexpensive transport throughout the island. Visitors can buy Singapore Explorer tickets, valid for one day or three days, at most leading hotels. If you pay your fare on the bus make sure you have the correct money, as no change is given on one-man operated buses. Bus guides are available at bookshops and SBS's head office at 205 Braddell Road. Hotline 287 2727.

The Singapore Trolley Bus service runs between Orchard Rd, Tanjong Pagar and World Trade Centre, 09:00–21:00. Ticket prices include discounts at local shops and some nightspots.

Taxis
Five companies operate more than 10,000 air-conditioned taxis, including London cabs, on the island. Watch out for surcharges (not indicated on meter) on: journeys between 00:00 and 06:00; telephone bookings and advance bookings; trips originating from the CBD (see below) between 16:00 and 19:00 (weekdays) and 12:00 and 15:00 (Sat); journeys to Changi Airport; purchase of an Area Licence for the CBD if the taxi is not already displaying one; hiring a London cab.

Note: Taxi drivers displaying red destination labels on their dashboard or windscreen are changing shifts and will only take passengers travelling in that general direction. Drivers may occasionally refuse to take passengers on journeys not convenient to them even if they are not changing shifts. If there is a taxi stand around, you must join the queue to get a taxi, otherwise it can be hailed anywhere.

Car rental
A costly way to travel in Singapore, where public transport is so efficient and parking expensive. Driving is on the left, seat-belts must be worn and the speed limit is

Singapore City at a Glance

50km/hr (80km/hr on express-ways).

Ken-Air Rent A Car, 277 Orchard Road, #01-41 Specialist Centre, tel 737 8282, fax 733 5513.

Ace Tours & Car Rental Pte Ltd, 37 Scotts Road, Asia Hotel, tel 235 3755, fax 235 6618.

Hertz Rent A Car, 125 Tanglin Road, Tudor Court Shopping Gallery, tel 734 4646, fax 345 7247.

Avis Rent A Car, 200 Orchard Boulevard, tel 737 1668

Central Business District (CBD)

The area around the Central Business District, Orchard Road and Chinatown is a restricted zone during rush hours. An Area Licence is needed to enter the CBD 07:30–10:15 and 16:30–18:30 Mon–Fri, 07:30–10:15 Sat. Daily licences are available from post offices or area licence booths. Monthly licences are also issued. Failure to display a licence incurs a fine.

WHERE TO STAY

Singapore has a wide choice of hotels catering for all budgets from the very luxurious to practical basic accommodation.

Luxury

Marina Mandarin Singapore, 6 Raffles Blvd, Marina Square, tel 338 3388, fax 339 4977. An architecturally interesting world-class hotel with a 21-storey atrium affording a splendid view of Marina Bay.

Four Seasons Hotel, 190 Orchard Blvd, tel 734 1110, fax 235 5131. A brand new ultra-chic hotel lavishly furnished with oriental antiques and works of art.

Goodwood Park Hotel, 22 Scotts Rd, tel 737 7411, fax 732 8558. An historic hotel with superb interior decoration complete with an old clock tower.

Raffles Hotel, 1 Beach Rd, tel 337 1886, fax 339 7650. The most famous historical landmark in Singapore, patronized by celebrities past and present. Suites only.

Hilton International Singapore, 581 Orchard Rd, tel 737 2233, fax 732 2917. Features newly renovated Executive Club; rooms furnished with business travellers in mind.

Shangri-la Hotel, 22 Orange Grove Rd, tel 737 3644, fax 733 7220. Established hotel with well-appointed rooms, popular with business travellers.

Upper mid-range

The Elizabeth, 24 Mt Elizabeth, tel 738 1188, fax 732 3866. Neo-classical architecture with a distinctive European decor; personalized service.

The Duxton, 83 Duxton Rd, tel 227 7678, fax 227 1232. Small traditional hotel converted from old Chinese shophouses with colonial decor in the heart of Tanjong Pagar.

York Hotel, 21 Mt Elizabeth, tel 737 0511, fax 732 1217. Quietly situated but within minutes' walk of Orchard Rd.

Le Meridien Singapore, 100 Orchard Rd, tel 733 8855, fax 732 7886. Smart shopping malls on the ground floor.

Lower mid-range

Hotel Equatorial Singapore, 429 Bukit Timah Rd, tel 732 0431, fax 737 9426. In an exclusive residential area within easy reach of Central Business District; complimentary shuttle-bus to Orchard Rd and Chinatown.

Ladyhill Hotel, 1 Ladyhill Road, tel 737 2111, fax 737 4606.

Cockpit Hotel, 6/7 Oxley Rise, tel 737 9111, fax 737 3105.

Cairnhill Hotel, 19 Cairnhill Circle, tel 734 6622, fax 235 5598.

Budget

Hotel Bencoolen, 47 Bencoolen St, tel 336 0822, fax 336 4384.

Mayfair City Hotel, 40/44 Armenian St, tel 337 4542, fax 337 1736.

Metropolitan YMCA, 60 Stevens Rd, tel 737 7755, fax 235 5528.

Sloane Court Hotel, 17 Balmoral Rd, tel 235 3311, fax 733 9041.

YWCA Hostel, 6/8 Fort Canning Rd, tel 336 1212, fax 737 3804.

Low-cost tourist hotels

Great Southern Hotel, 70–78A/B, Eu Tong Sen St, tel

Singapore City at a Glance

533 3223.

Lido Hotel, 54/56 Middle Rd, tel 337 1872.

Mitre Hotel, 145 Killiney Rd, tel 737 3811.

Peony Mansion Travellers' Lodge, 46 Bencoolen St, #04-46, Peony Mansion, tel 338 5638.

WHERE TO EAT

Singapore's restaurants are legion, so this is a tiny selection.

Chinese

Inn of Happiness, Hilton International Singapore, 581 Orchard Rd, tel 737 2233. Cantonese; speciality: claypot dishes.

House of Blossoms, Marina Mandarin Singapore, 6 Raffles Blvd, Marina Square, tel 338 3388. Cantonese and Teochew; speciality: barbecued Beijing duck.

Golden Phoenix Sichuan Restaurant, Hotel Equatorial Singapore, 429 Bukit Timah Rd, tel 732 0431. Renowned for its superb Sichuan dishes.

Prosperity House, Clarke Quay, 3E River Valley Rd, #01-09, tel 334 1983. Shanghainese; speciality: seafood claypot.

Lingzhi Vegetarian Restaurant, 400 Orchard Rd, #B1-17/18 Orchard Towers, tel 734 3788.

Dollars Restaurant, 160 Orchard Rd, #B1-02 Orchard Pt, tel 738 9688. Hong Kong dim sum and other value-for-money dishes.

Pine Court, 35th Floor Main Wing, Mandarin Singapore, 333 Orchard Rd, tel 831 6262. Speciality: classic Beijing duck.

Indian

Sasurai, 39 Campbell Lane, tel 336 9100. North Indian; specialities: biryanis and tandoori dishes.

Sonargaon Restaurant, 18 Cuff Rd, tel 299 9960. Bangladeshi; specialities: chicken roast masala, bhoona mutton and pangas curry.

Bagavathy Eating House, 37 Chander Rd, tel 299 1197. South Indian; specialities: kurma chicken, mutton and vegetarian dishes.

Velu's Curry Fish Head, 11 Stanley St, tel 221 1115. Specialities: fish head deluxe and masala dishes.

Babataher Café & Restaurant, Lau Pa Sat, 18 Raffles Quay R-7, tel 222 4732. North Indian; specialities: Muglai dishes and butter chicken.

Malay and Indonesian

Tradewinds Restaurant, Hilton International Singapore, 531 Orchard Rd, tel 730 3395. Poolside alfresco barbecue.

Restoran Temenggung, 895 Geylang Serai Malay Village, tel 748 4700.

Sanur Indonesian Restaurant, #04-16 Takashimaya Shopping Centre, Ngee Ann City, tel 734 3434. Specialities: Sanur fish head and tahu telur.

Sayna Indonesian Restaurant, Clarke Quay, 3D River Valley Rd, #01-04, tel 339 6388. Fiery traditional Indonesian cuisine.

Nonya

Nonya and Baba, 262 River Valley Rd, tel 734 1382.

Thai

Baan Thai, #04-23 Takashimaya Shopping Centre, Ngee Ann City, tel 735 5562. Specialities: charcoal grilled fish in Thai spices and baked king prawn with vermicelli in a pot.

Thanying Restaurant, Clarke Quay, Blk D, River Valley Rd, #04-14, tel 735 5562.

Western

Ristorante Bologna, Marina Mandarin Singapore, 4th Level, 6 Raffles Blvd, tel 331 8470. Speciality: seabass fillet with porcini.

Hot Stones Steak & Seafood Restaurant, The Dinosaurs Restaurant, No 53 Boat Quay, tel 534 5188. Specialities: prawn quesadilla and steak cooked on heated stones.

5 Emerald Hill Bar & Restaurant, 5 Emerald Hill, tel 732 0818. Restored shophouse. Specialities: T-bone steak and salmon steak.

La Brasserie, Omni Marco Polo Hotel, Tanglin Rd, tel 474 7141. Specialities: crispy duck à l'orange and beef bourguignon.

The Greenhouse Dining Room, The Elizabeth, 24 Mt Elizabeth, tel 738 1188. Western and Asian; specialities: black pepper steak and

Singapore City at a Glance

fish and chips.
Japanese
Tonkichi, #04-24
Takashimaya Shopping
Centre, Ngee Ann City, tel
735 7522. Tonkatsu menu.
Restaurant Hoshigaoka,
Centrepoint Branch, #03-
45/46, 176 Orchard Rd, tel
734 0259.
**Kampachi Japanese
Restaurant**, Hotel Equatorial
Singapore, 429 Bukit Timah
Rd, tel 732 0431.
**Kekayi Japanese
Restaurant**, Pan Pacific Hotel,
Level 4, 7 Raffles Blvd, Marina
Square, tel 336 8111.
Specialities: sushi, sashimi,
teppanyaki and tempura.
Afternoon tea
Very popular in Singapore,
especially on Sundays, and
offered by all the major
hotels.
Upstairs, Tudor Court, 145A
Tanglin Rd, tel 732 3922.
Cream teas in traditional
English restaurant.
Goodwood Park Hotel, 22
Scotts Rd, tel 737 7411.
Buffet tea served on the lawn.
Hawker Centres
Hawkers Alley, Clarke Quay,
River Valley Rd.
Bugis Street, Bugis Village.
Cuppage Centre, 55
Cuppage Rd, off Orchard Rd.
**Chinatown Complex
Hawker Centre**, Block 335,
1st Floor, Smith St.
Bars/Pubs/Nightclubs
Fiesta Wine Bar, Lorong
Mambong, Holland Village.
Long Bar, Levels 2 & 3,
Raffles Hotel Arcade, 1 Beach

Rd, tel 337 1886.
Flag and Whistle, 10 Duxton
Hill. A traditional English pub.
**Ozzee 103 Dance Pub and
Café**, Clarke Quay, 3A River
Valley Rd.
Bar and Billard Room,
Raffles Hotel Arcade, 1 Beach
Rd, tel 337 1886. Live jazz
nightly.
Boom Boom Room, Bugis
Village, tel 339 8187. Late-
night cabaret.
Hard Rock Café, 50
Cuscaden Rd, tel 235 5232.

TOURS AND EXCURSIONS

Singapore's tour operators
offer a wide variety of organized trips around the city,
either for general sightseeing
or with a special interest.
Evening tours include a meal,
usually at an open-air food
centre. Bookings can be made
with the companies or
through your hotel tour desk.
There is also a wide choice of
tours outside the city: see
page 99 for some suggestions.
Tour Operators
Holiday Tours and Travel,
tel 738 2622, fax 733 3226.
RMG Tours, tel 738 7776,
fax 235 5256.
**Singapore Sightseeing
Tour East**, tel 235 5703, fax
235 1075.

Nam Ho Travel, tel 221
8433, fax 225 2588.
**River and Island Cruises
Eastwind Organization**, tel
533 3432, fax 534 2533.
Singapore River Cruises, tel
227 6863, fax 227 7287.
Waterfront Cruises, tel 532
4497, fax 235 5266.
Fantasy Cruises, tel 284
0424, fax 382 5293.

USEFUL CONTACTS

**Singapore Tourist
Promotion Board (STPB)**,
Head Office: Raffles City
Tower, #36-04, 250 North
Bridge Rd, Singapore 0617,
tel 339 6622, fax 339 9423.
**Tourist Information
Centres**: Raffles Hotel
Arcade, #02-34, 328 North
Bridge Rd, tel 1800 334
1335/6 (toll free); open daily
08:30–18:00.
Scotts Shopping Centre, #02-
03, Scotts Rd, tel 1800 738
3778/9 (toll free); open daily
09:30–21:30.
General Post Office,
Fullerton Rd, off Collyer Quay
and Battery Rd.
National Library, Stamford
Rd (next to National
Museum).
Comcentre (main public tele-
phone office), 31 Exeter Rd;
open 24 hrs.

SINGAPORE	J	F	M	A	M	J	J	A	S	O	N	D
AVERAGE TEMP. °F	78	79	80	80	81	82	81	80	80	80	79	78
AVERAGE TEMP. °C	26	26	27	27	27	27	27	27	27	27	26	26
Hours of Sun Daily	5	5	6	6	6	6	6	6	5	5	4	4
RAINFALL "	9	7	7	7	7	6	6	7	7	8	10	11
RAINFALL mm	239	167	186	180	173	166	159	178	176	197	258	280
Days of Rainfall	15	11	14	15	15	13	13	14	14	16	19	20

3
The South and West

To the south and west of the city of Singapore you will find a variety of interesting places to visit, from wildlife parks and gardens to themed attractions. All are well served by MRT stations and buses. Jurong is Singapore's principal industrial area, employing two-thirds of the country's industrial workforce. However, a number of tourist attractions have been created amongst the housing estates.

DON'T MISS

** The bustling streets and shops of **Holland Village**.
** The astonishing world of science at the **Singapore Science Centre**.
*** **Jurong Bird Park**, with the world's largest aviary.
** The beauty and tranquillity of the **Chinese** and **Japanese Gardens**.
** Lunch or dinner at the elegant **Alkaff Mansion** with a panoramic view of the harbour.

Singapore Botanic Gardens ***

Close to the city, not far from the top end of Orchard Road, the Botanic Gardens in Cluny Road were founded in 1859, and now provide a green refuge for those wanting to escape from the suffocating city atmosphere. Covering an area of 52ha (130 acres), vistas of rolling green lawns are punctuated with bursts of colour from a profusion of orchids and other flowering plants. The gardens' orchidarium displays 250 orchid species and hybrids. In contrast, the landscape includes the green canopy of areas of primary forest with their huge diversity of plant species.

In 1877, these gardens saw the origin of the Malayan rubber industry when Henry Ridley planted 11 Brazilian rubber tree seedlings propagated in London's Kew Gardens. There is a memorial to Ridley, who was director of the gardens from 1888 to 1912, on the spot where the original trees were planted.

The landscape is further enhanced by the lakes, inhabited by carp, waterfowl and kingfishers. Outdoor

Opposite: *The green open spaces of the Botanic Gardens offer a tranquil respite from the city heat.*

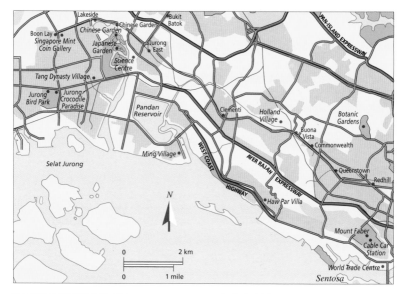

As well as several orchids that grow naturally on Singapore, an enormous number of species and hybrids are nurtured here. The orchidarium at the Botanic Gardens includes some rareties among its 250 varieties, as well as the *Vanda* Miss Joachim. This bright purple hybrid, which was chosen as the 'national flower' in 1981, was found in the garden of Agnes Joachim as a chance seedling in 1893.

You can enjoy a panoramic view of the harbour from the terrace of the elegant Alkaff Mansion.

concerts are regularly held here, while newly-weds frequently make a beeline for the most scenic spot in the gardens for photo shoots.

The gardens are open from 5:00 to 23:00 on weekdays and 5:00 to 00:00 on weekends and public holidays.

Holland Village ★★

This small suburban shopping centre on Holland Road, which runs west from Orchard Road, has long been a hub of activity for the expatriate community as well as the locals. It is especially crowded at weekends, when the various communities converge here to browse in the many shops selling anything from bric-à-brac, antiques and crafts to electronic goods and clothing. Bargain-hunting is the order of the day, and you can find good souvenirs here, such as embroidered silk or cloisonné ware. Here the old Singapore jostles with modernity, as the wet market and the traditional shophouses nestle amongst ritzy wine bars and fancy restaurants. It is a place full of interest with a true village atmosphere, away from the pressure of Orchard Road.

Mount Faber *

Perched off Telok Blangah Road, the undulating ridges of Mount Faber enclose a tranquil residential area with manicured gardens. At the peak of the hill, a look-out building offers a panoramic vista of the harbour and Sentosa Island, which can be reached by cable car from the station here. Souvenir shops occupy the two floors of the building and Indian snake charmers in the courtyard try to coax visitors to pose for photographs with the reptiles coiled round their necks in return for a small fee. There is little to do or see here apart from admiring the view, though if you have time a buffet lunch at the Alkaff Mansion nearby is a very pleasant way to savour the serenity of Mount Faber.

Alkaff Mansion **

Originally known as Mount Washington, the Alkaff Mansion was the home of a wealthy Arab family in the 1920s. The first Alkaff, Syed Shaik, came to Singapore in 1852 to join his brother Mohammed in the spice trade with the East India Company. By 1923, the Alkaffs were among the wealthiest families in Singapore, with a diversity of business interests. Amongst the many houses they owned was this mansion built on Mount Faber Ridge, commanding a panoramic view of Singapore Harbour. It was lovingly restored to its former splendour in 1988 and was earmarked as an historic building. Today it is an

RUBBER RIDLEY

Henry Nicholas Ridley, an English botanist, was appointed the first director of the Singapore Botanic Gardens in 1888. He spent the next 25 years ardently developing the gardens into an international centre for the study of tropical plants and their economic application.

His research convinced him that the Brazilian Para rubber tree (*Hevea brasiliensis*) had great commercial value. He tried to persuade the government to grow the trees on a large scale in Malaya, with its ideal climate, but was met with strong opposition and was dubbed 'Mad Ridley' or 'Rubber Ridley' by his detractors. Undeterred, he pursued his conviction with great fervour and eventually drew international interest in the gardens through his many publications. The first rubber tree seedlings were despatched to the Botanic Gardens in 1877 from Kew in England, where 70,000 seeds had been shipped from the Amazon forest for germination. Ridley used every opportunity to persuade Malayan planters to give this crop a trial and succeeded in convincing the first few by 1896. He also refined the 'herring-bone' method of tapping rubber which remains unchanged today. By 1920 Malaya was producing more than half the world's rubber and Singapore had become a major centre for the trade.

GAMBIER

By 1819 there were already about twenty Chinese gambier plantations on Singapore. An abundance of firewood from the rainforest was used to provide fuel for the boiling of the gambier leaves. In the 1830s, soaring demand from the British tanning and dyeing industries sent up the price and encouraged Chinese farmers to cultivate new plantations further inland to the north and west. By the 1840s there were 600 plantations employing about 6000 Chinese labourers, but ten years later the soil was exhausted and the forest depleted. The plundered land gave way to coarse elephant grass and by 1867 much of the interior of the island was a wasted and desolate tract.

Cruises to the southern islands depart from the World Trade Centre.

elegant restaurant and is a popular venue for entertaining and weddings. A winding road leads to the majestic building, approached by a grand white staircase. In the reception area the original floral tiles of grey and dark green have been meticulously preserved. The interior of polished wood and beams is furnished with antiques from the 1920s, and the large garden is beautifully landscaped with indigenous plants and fruit trees.

World Trade Centre **

At the southernmost tip of the island, opposite Sentosa, lies the focal point of the maritime activities of Singapore. The World Trade Centre (WTC) adjoining the **Singapore Cruise Centre** is the departure point for cruise liners and ferries to Indonesia and the islands of Singapore. The whole complex also doubles as a family fun centre and entertainment plaza, with an amphitheatre, restaurants, shops, travel agents, banks and attractions like the **Guinness World of Records Exhibition** and **Maritime Showcase**. At weekends, the **Harbour Market** bustles with stalls selling curios and crafts. Dining or strolling along the breezy **Harbour Promenade** affords a view of the busy port: blasts from their horns announce the ships' departures and catamarans skim over the ocean to distant islands.

The Guinness World of Records Exhibition ★★

Situated in Maritime Square at the World Trade Centre, this exhibition is a visual display based on the *Guinness Book of World Records*. Three-dimensional life-size replicas, audio presentations and interactive exhibits present the world's extremes: the fattest, thinnest, biggest, smallest, fastest, oldest and bravest. The exhibition is open from 10:00 to 19:00 on weekdays and 09:30 to 19:00 at weekends and public holidays.

Singapore Maritime Showcase ★★

This educational and entertaining attraction on Harbour Promenade at WTC takes visitors on a maritime odyssey through time from the early days of Singapore as a small fishing port to its present day and the projection of the port into the 21st century. The **Technodrome** features state-of-the-art three-dimensional graphics and computer animation in the movie *Over the Horizon* while on board the *Neptune Topaz* you can travel to famous seaports such as Rotterdam and New York as well as Singapore. Other exhibits display the wonders of the ocean. Watch out for the biggest Lego models on display in Singapore. Opening times: 11:00 to 20:00 (closed on Monday), 11:00 to 21:00 on Saturdays and eve of public holidays.

Haw Par Villa Dragon World ★★

This theme park in Pasir Panjang Road is the Disneyland of the East. It was formerly known as Tiger Balm Gardens, named after the famous 'cure-all-aches' ointment which made the fortune of the Aw brothers, the creators of the original garden which opened in 1937. It has now been revamped and renamed, and is a lively entertainment park, graphically portraying 5000 years of Chinese mythology and

> **MIRACLE CURE**
>
> The ubiquitous Tiger Balm is an essential item in the medicine cabinet of most Singaporean families. This 'cure-all' ointment made the fortune and fame of the Aw brothers, Boon Haw and Boon Par. The original concoction was the brainchild of their herbalist father, Aw Chu Kin, who bequeathed them the recipe, which includes 'menthol, camphor, clove oil, peppermint oil, cajuput oil, paraffin and petrolatum'. Singaporeans swear by it for the relief of insect bites, toothache, and all manner of minor aches and pains. Aw Boon Par, who founded the Chinese newspaper *Sin Chiew Jit Poh* in 1929, was a major influence among the Hakka and Cantonese population. His fame earned him the nickname 'Tiger Balm King'.

Enter the dragon's jaws at Haw Par Villa for a chastening journey through the Ten Courts of Hell.

The Chinese Garden, on an island in Jurong Lake, is dotted with buildings in the style of the Sung Dynasty.

legends in the form of gaudy tableaux and rides with moralistic themes such as love, duty, patience, charity, honesty and luck. In addition there are theatrical events, pageants and puppet shows about history, legends and heroes, including a three-dimensional show on the Chinese interpretation of the Creation of the World, lion dances and a ride into the dragon's mouth to see the harrowing scenes of the 'Ten Courts of Hell', illustrating the punishments meted out to earthly evil-doers in the afterlife.

The park opens daily from 09:00 to 18:00. Allow about three hours for your visit, and try to avoid busy times, especially Chinese New Year.

New Ming Village *

This village at Pandan Road demonstrates and reproduces the ancient art of porcelain-making of the Ming and Qing dynasties, which produced the finest porcelain in the history of China. Visitors can watch skilled artisans at work using the age-old techniques of calligraphy and motif-painting on reproductions of the porcelain. The finished products are for sale in the showroom. It is open every day from 09:00 to 17:30.

Singapore Science Centre **

Located in the aptly named Science Centre Road, this 'hands-on' museum with 600 exhibits and interactive displays brings fun and entertainment to the world of science. It is chiefly aimed at children, many of whom visit in school parties, but its imaginative explanations of scientific principles are just as appealing to adults. Its highlights include the **Aviation Gallery** which charts the history and principles of flight; the **Omnimax Theatre**

FISHY BUSINESS

According to a 1992 report, the total annual supply of fresh fish, farm-bred or caught locally, amounted to 11,547 tonnes. Local fishermen use three main methods: trawling, gill-netting and long-lining. There are wholesale markets at Jurong and Punggol; the Jurong Fish Market also serves as a docking and bunkering base for foreign fishing vessels operating in this region. Factories nearby provide fish processing, ice-making and cold storage services. In Changi, the Marine Aquaculture Section researches and advises on farm management and fish husbandry. Ornamental fish exported during 1992 were worth S$70.5 million.

which gives the viewer a virtual reality experience of the films projected on its massive hemispherical screen with special sound effects; and the **Planetarium Show** taking visitors on an excursion around the solar system. The centre is open from 10:00 to 18:00 (closed on Monday). There are separate admission fees for entrance to the museum, the Omnimax Theatre and the Planetarium Show (check the times of shows locally).

Mint Coin Gallery
Chinese Garden
Japanese Garden
Science Centre
Jurong
New Ming Village
Haw Par Villa

Chinese and Japanese Gardens **

These two gardens are set on adjacent islands in Jurong Lake at Yuan Ching Road, and are linked to each other by the 'Bridge of Double Beauty'. They exemplify the contrasting garden architecture of the two cultures. The Chinese Garden, known locally as **Yu Hwa Yuan**, is fashioned after an imperial Sung dynasty design and mimics the grandeur of the Beijing Summer Palace. The landscape includes ornamental buildings with poetic names like 'Cloud-Piercing Pagoda', 'Moon-Receiving Tower' and 'Jade-Splashed Bridge'. Streams and pools such as the 'Fragrance-Filled Lily Pond' are dotted with vermilion and gold pavilions and stone boats. It is a favourite with bridal parties seeking romantic photographic locations for their wedding albums.

By contrast, the Japanese Garden or **Seiwaen**, the 'Garden of Tranquillity', is refreshingly serene. Carp ponds are spanned by wooden bridges, the landscape is traversed by pebble footpaths and stone lanterns are carefully placed amongst the shrubberies. It is a congenial place for those seeking peace and poetic inspiration.

The gardens are open from 09:00 to 19:00 Monday to Saturday; 08:30 to 19:00 on Sundays and public holidays.

Singapore Mint Coin Gallery *

Not far from the Chinese and Japanese Gardens at 249 Jalan Boon Lay is the numismatic museum of Singapore, where coins, medals and medallions from all over the world are displayed. Visitors can mint their own souvenir coin in the gallery's coin press. Open Monday to Friday only from 09:00 to 16:00.

OPIUM

In the early 1900s, opium addiction was a major cause of the high mortality and ill health amongst the Chinese immigrants of Singapore. Whilst the habit was a fairly harmless indulgence among the rich it was deleterious to the poor who could afford to smoke only the dregs of used opium. Addiction was notably widespread among the rickshaw pullers, whose life expectancy rarely exceeded 35 or 40 years. A campaign was launched to discourage the smoking of opium and in 1906, the Singapore Anti-Opium Society was founded and a rehabilitation centre was established. This met with opposition from most European and Chinese merchants and farmers, who saw their revenue from opium declining. The government was caught in a moral and financial dilemma and in 1910, as a compromise, took over the manufacturing and sale of opium. A government factory was set up at Pasir Panjang. Opium could only be purchased under licence and this eventually eliminated the problem.

PASIR PANJANG

Pasir Panjang ('Long Sand' in Malay) played an important role in the Japanese occupation of Singapore. This coastal region in the west was populated mostly by Malays in the 1930s when shipping and business interests began to develop in nearby Telok Blangah. The Malay population earned their living from fishing, charcoal-burning and driving bullock carts in the harbour area. Friday 13 February 1942 was an unlucky day for the defending forces during the onslaught of the Japanese army on the western flank of the island. The C Company of the 1st Battalion, Malay Regiment began a 48-hour defence against the advancing Japanese army on Bukit Chandu (also known as Opium Hill due to the presence of the government opium factory), a natural ridge running behind Pasir Panjang fishing village. Despite a fierce and brave resistance, the Japanese broke through Pasir Panjang Ridge and only when the last man of the garrison was wiped out did the defence fail. The heavily populated town which sprawled behind the front line was now at the mercy of the Imperial Army.

Tang Dynasty City **

Situated off Yuan Ching Road, this is Asia's largest historical and cultural theme park, recreating **Chang-An**, the capital of the Tang dynasty of 7th-century China. Chinese art and culture flourished during this period and the park attempts to portray this aspect faithfully. All the building materials, as well as the skilled artisans who recreated the city, have been imported from China. To complete the effect, the whole city is surrounded by the **Great Wall of China**. Inside, the city is a hive of activity, with the **Silk Road Market Place** crowded by merchants, inns serving tea and shops selling souvenirs and Chinese medicine. There are re-enactments of wedding processions and Chinese epics, with duelling swordsmen 'walking on water' to save damsels in distress. There are also martial arts demonstrations and acrobatic acts. The **Underground Palace** houses life-sized replicas of the renowned terracotta warriors at Xian in China, while the **Shui Lian Cave** evokes the birthplace of the Monkey God. The city doubles as a movie set for classical and kung-fu films. For refreshment, there is a café serving buffet meals in addition to the **Tai He Lou Theatre Restaurant** which stages performances by classical Chinese dancers and acrobats.

Tang Dynasty City is open daily from 09:30 to 18:30.

Jurong Bird Park ***

This park on Jalan Ahmad Ibrahim claims to contain the world's largest and most impressive aviaries, covering an area of 20ha (50 acres). It is home to 7000 birds of 600 species, displayed in huge enclosures. Before starting your tour it is advisable to take an orientation trip on the **Panorail**, the air-conditioned monorail system which affords an overview of the entire park with a running commentary pointing out the main attractions. Using the park's map, a walking tour is recommended to appreciate properly the wonderful collections of the feathered kind. Don't miss the bird show in the **Pools Amphitheatre**, with colourful macaws, owls, eagles and condors, and the **Penguin Parade** enclosure in a carefully air-conditioned

The 'Panorail' takes visitors around Jurong Bird Park, so that you can be sure you will not miss any of this spectacular avian collection in its beautiful setting.

Antarctic setting with 200 penguins of five species and 50 seabirds. The **Walk-in Aviary** is a must with its 2ha (5 acre) netted enclosure, complete with a man-made waterfall and 100 species of free-flying tropical birds in a naturalistic habitat. The park claims to have the biggest collections of hornbills and South American toucans in the world. There is a simulated tropical thunderstorm daily at midday. If you are an 'early bird' you can have breakfast on the **Songbird Terrace** to the accompaniment of the singing birds. Check the times of bird shows and feeding times locally; the park is open from 09:00 to 18:00 from Monday to Saturday, and from 08:00 to 18:00 on Sunday and public holidays.

Jurong Crocodile Paradise *

Situated next door to Jurong Bird Park, this crocodile farm is certainly no paradise for the reptiles, which are reared for their skin. While waiting in 'death-row', the creatures are reluctant foils for the keepers' performances in death-defying acts of crocodile wrestling and handling. The farm has over 2500 crocodiles living in a recreation of their natural habitat, with an underwater viewing gallery and breeding enclosures where nests of eggs are fiercely guarded by their mothers. Whilst the skins are used for making handbags and shoes, the crocodile meat ends up on the menu of the restaurant in the main entrance building. The Chinese credit crocodile meat with medicinal value, especially in the treatment of asthma. The farm is open daily from 09:00 to 18:00; check the times for shows and feeding locally.

JURONG

In 1961 the Economic Development Board set up an industrial estate with the reclamation of 1600ha (4000 acres) of wasteland and swamp, aided by the World Bank. It failed to attract new industries however, due to political instability during the formation of Malaysia and confrontation with Indonesia. When the situation settled down in the late 1960s, industrialists and foreign investors once more began to show interest in Singapore. From 1968, manufacturing activities began to speed up and the area was reorganized into Jurong Town Corporation which today manages 30 industrial estates in various parts of the island. The 5825ha (14,500 acre) Jurong industrial estates maintain a high standard of town planning, engineering and real estate management. They support some 4500 companies, employing a total of 276,700 workers.

4
The East Coast and Changi

The eastern region of Singapore used to be considered the rural area of the country. Lush greenery clothed most of the landscape, dotted with Malay villages on stilts shaded by coconut palms and fruit trees. Today, the east coast has taken on a different character after a major facelift involving land reclamation and development schemes. The villages have been replaced by low-cost modern HDB flats, with terraces of houses and individual villas for the more well-heeled. Reclaimed land forms most of the **East Coast Parkway** which is lined with leisure facilities including the **East Coast Recreation Centre**, the **East Coast Sailing Club** and the **Wet and Wild** water park. The man-made beach is dotted with seafood restaurants. The **Geylang** and **Katong** districts remain a stronghold for the Malay and Peranakan communities. At the eastern end of the island lie **Changi Airport**, the nation's ultra-modern international airport, **Changi Beach** and **Village** and **Changi Prison**.

DON'T MISS

** The atmospheric Malay districts of **Geylang** and **Katong**.
** The evocation of wartime Singapore under Japanese occupation at **Changi Prison Museum**.
* The quiet rustic setting of **Changi Village** and the many attractions along **East Coast Road**.

Geylang and Katong Districts **

Once a lemon grass plantation, Geylang is the traditional domain of the Muslim population of Singapore: Malay, Indonesian and Arab communities all live here. A visit to Geylang and its many lanes where market trading continues to thrive can still evoke the atmosphere of old Singapore. Here, shops sell gems from Burma, spices, cotton and gold from India and rattan products from Indonesia, while the musky scent of Arabian perfume hangs in the air. Stroll down **Joo Chiat Road** (off

Opposite: *Malay fishermen use this traditional trap, known as a* kelong, *to lure their catch into a net submerged beneath the structure.*

PROMINENT ARABS OF OLD SINGAPORE

Arab traders played an important part in the shaping of Singapore. They settled in the Arab Street area and the Muslim district of Geylang. Three prominent families were the Alkaffs, the Alsagoffs and the Al-Junieds. They were all philanthropists, building hospitals, schools and mosques and sponsoring religious festivals.

The Al-Junieds had established themselves in Southeast Asia long before Raffles set foot in Singapore. The first Al-Junieds to arrive on the island in 1819 were Syed Mohammed bin Harun and his nephew, Syed Omar bin Ali, wealthy merchants from Palembang in Sumatra. Syed Shaik bin Abdul Rahman Alkaff, arrived in 1852 from Indonesia to join his brother, Mohammed, in the spice trade. By 1923 they owned 99 houses and other buildings, amongst which were the Arcade on the waterfront at Collyer Quay, and Alkaff Mansion.

The Alsagoffs owned several properties, including the old bungalow at the corner of Beach and Bras Basah Roads which was bought by the Sarkies brothers. It was to become the most famous landmark in Singapore: Raffles Hotel.

Geylang Road) for a fascinating glimpse of the Chinese community here with its joss stick and candle-making industries. On the site of an old coconut plantation, this area abounds with textile merchants, with every display space awash with shimmering silk, colourful batik and gaudy rugs. It is a bargain-hunter's paradise. For local cuisine, try one of the many Malay restaurants or food centres where *nasi padang*, a West Sumatran dish of curried meat and vegetables served with rice, is a speciality.

Adjacent to Geylang is the **Katong** district, where wealthy Peranakan families once resided in seaside villas. Sadly, the sea view is now impeded by modern apartment blocks on reclaimed land. This quiet residential suburb with its relaxed atmosphere presents a change of pace from bustling downtown Singapore. Whilst the shoreline may have been moved further away through reclamation, the nostalgic ambience of this former seaside town lingers on. There are very attractive Peranakan shophouses with colourful façades and shuttered windows along **Koon Seng Road**, just off Joo Chiat Road on the left. These magnificent buildings have been lovingly restored to enhance the beautiful plasterwork depicting fruits, flowers and animals with motif tiles. Look out for the bat-shaped air vents on the front walls of the houses: these serve the double purpose of provid-

Dazzling traditional Malay outfits fill a shop in Geylang Serai, Singapore's Muslim heartland.

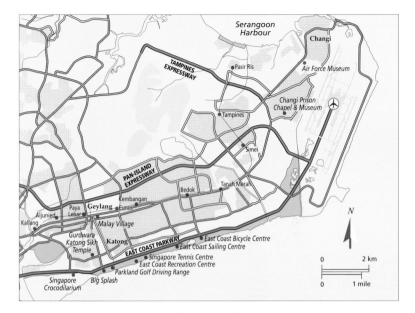

ing ventilation and bringing good luck to the house, since the Chinese word for bat, *fu*, also means fortune and happiness.

As befits its heritage, Katong is famous for its Peranakan restaurants and coffee shops which sell delicious curry puffs – pastries filled with curried minced meat and vegetables. Some of the shophouses along East Coast Road offer magnificent Chinese seafood.

Malay Village *

Situated in Geylang Serai in the Geylang district, this recently created showcase of Malay culture is a low-rise complex featuring Malay restaurants, ethnic goods, arts and crafts. Best buys are souvenirs, antiques, paintings, clothes and accessories.

The Singapore Crocodilarium *

At 730 East Coast Parkway, this is a crocodile farm where the reptiles are reared for their skin. While waiting to be turned into bags and accessories, the crocodiles

---

AN AROMATIC PAST

'Serai' is the local name for lemon grass, a characteristic ingredient of Southeast Asian cooking, and Geylang Serai was once the site of a lemon grass plantation. Mills in the area processed the crop to produce citronella, the fragrant essential oil used in perfumery.

The seascape is always full of activity off the beaches of the east coast.

double up as a tourist attraction, wrestling with their keepers to amuse visitors. There are over 1000 crocodiles here and they can be viewed at close range. The farm is open daily from 09:00 to 17:00, and feeding-time is at 11:00 every Tuesday, Thursday and Saturday. Crocodile skin products are on sale in the souvenir shop.

Singapore Air Force Museum ★

This museum, at Block 78, Cranwell Road, off Loyang Avenue near Changi, charts the history of the Republic of Singapore Air Force from its formation as the Malayan Volunteer Air Force in 1939 to the present day. The museum houses a vast collection of military artefacts and flying machines including early planes like the Hunter Hawker, the SF 260 Marchetti and the A4-C Skyhawk. There is also a display of colonial cap badges and the Bloodhound missile. For war relics enthusiasts, it makes an interesting visit. Opening times are 10:00 to 16:30 (closed on Mondays and public holidays).

Changi Prison Chapel and Museum ★

Situated on Upper Changi Road North, next to the prison, the open-air chapel is a simple wooden affair with a thatched roof over the altar. It is a replica, constructed by inmates of the prison, of the original chapel built by Allied prisoners of war in World War II. In the face of adversity and the hopelessness of their situation, the chapel became the focal point of the prisoners' lives as they turned to religion to sustain their spirits. To the right of the outdoor pews is a large notice which encourages visitors to pick flowers from the hibiscus and other flowering shrubs by the chapel and to place them on the altar to honour those who died. On the left wall of the chapel is a notice board where visitors who lost friends or relatives in the war can pin little cards with moving messages of remembrance for their dear departed. The war may be long over but it will always be remembered in the poignant words of a Far East Prisoner of War prayer:

And we that are left grow old with the years
Remembering the heartache, the pain and the tears;
Hoping and praying that never again
Man will sink to such sorrow and shame.
The price that was paid we will always remember,
Every day, every month, not just in November.

Adjacent to the chapel is the museum, in which vivid accounts of the harrowing experiences of the prisoners of war are illustrated with photographs and paintings. It is an emotional experience to walk round the museum imagining the inhumanity and degradation these prisoners suffered at the hands of the Japanese during the occupation. Changi Prison, which was built to house 600 prisoners, was used to intern 3500 civilian men, women and children after the Allied surrender.

The museum is open from 09:30 to 16:30 (closed on Sundays and public holidays). There is a service in the chapel each Sunday at 17:30.

INSIDE CHANGI PRISON

During the Second World War Changi Prison was used to intern civilian prisoners in harrowing and degrading conditions. Originally built for 600, it became the home of 12,000 internees, 5000 in the building itself and the rest in makeshift campsites around it. In the face of starvation, cruel treatment and disease, an indomitable and innovative spirit sustained the morale of the prisoners. Women prisoners would convey word of their survival to the outside world by embroidering their names on quilts intended for Allied prisoners. To keep themselves occupied the prisoners organized lectures on various subjects from Shakespeare to foreign languages. From rubber latex, coagulated with urine, they created soles for shoes, while paper was made from grass, water and potash. Artificial limbs for amputee prisoners were fashioned out of old filing cabinets and wood from the rubber trees. They grew vegetables to supplement their near-starvation diet and boiled sea-water for salt. Diseases such as ulcers, beriberi and dystentery were rampant. The prisoners found comfort in religion and built a small atap chapel for their daily prayers.

Changi Prison Chapel, a replica of the simple thatched wooden structure erected by Allied prisoners during World War II.

Changi Village, far from the bustle of urban Singapore, offers gentle pursuits such as a day on the beach or a relaxed meal on a shady terrace.

MALAY FISHING TRAPS

A traditional Malay method of catching fish is to set up a trap known as a *kelong*, looking like a wooden hut on thin legs. A fence of stakes channels the fish towards the trap and into a huge net hung just below the surface of the water. When full, it is winched up onto the platform. *Kelong* are used to catch the little anchovies which, when dried, are a vital element of Malay cuisine.

Changi Beach and Village ★

On the eastern tip of the East Coast region, Changi Village is a small quiet settlement. The main village square has a food centre serving local dishes, flanked by shops catering mainly for the local community. A few restaurants and souvenir shops are scattered along the road. For a real thirst quencher, sample the cool refreshing juice of a young green coconut (ask the vendor for a spoon to scoop out its delicious tender flesh to complete the treat).

Changi Beach bears silent witness to the execution of thousands of civilians by the Japanese army of occupation. It is a clean stretch of sand mostly frequented by the locals, especially at weekends. The water, though not particularly tempting, is popular with bathers and fishermen, who set up large elevated fish traps called *kelong*. Bumboats, cargo ships and supertankers fill up the seascape like carelessly parked cars while Peninsular Malaysia looms in the distance.

Changi Airport

Dominating the eastern end of the island is Singapore's international airport. The site on which it stands was cleared of coconut plantations to become a British naval and air-force base in 1926. Changi became an international airport in 1981, and its second terminal was completed in 1991. Voted the best airport in the world, it has been called 'a global hub that is a destination in itself'. Transiting here can be sweet agony when you are faced with over 100 shops, a free two-hour city sightseeing tour to join and a flight to catch. There are over 20 restaurants and bars, 100 day rooms, gym, sauna, health centre, two fully equipped business centres, a free mini-cinema screening the latest blockbusters, and much more. For children, there is a 'science discovery corner' and nursery with play area.

The airport is very clean and user-friendly with clear signs and a comprehensive floor-plan. Orchids and tropical gardens with fountains and ornamental ponds complete with carp decorate the departure and transit lounge, where the resident pianist entertains you as you sip your cocktail. Changi handles over 2650 flights a week and boasts that passengers can collect and clear their baggage through customs in 20 minutes.

THE VERSATILE COCONUT PALM

Every part of the ubiquitous coconut palm has a use in Southeast Asia. The trunk is used for flooring or walls while the leaves make cool practical roofs and shelter. The ribs of the leaves are fashioned into brooms and satay sticks, the leaves woven into baskets, hats, and mats.

The *pièce de résistance* of the palm is the nut itself. Eaten young, the green nut is full of delicious sweet juice which is a real thirst-quencher in the tropics and the delectable tender flesh melts in the mouth. When matured, the kernel is delicious eaten raw and produces copra for oil; when grated it yields rich coconut milk, an indispensable ingredient in Southeast Asian cuisine.

The husk of the coconut is made into brooms, floor polishers, containers, matting and is useful as hanging baskets for growing orchids. The hard shells of the nuts make excellent containers, ash trays, ladles, ornaments and jewellery.

Proud of its reputation as the world's best airport, Changi offers so many facilities that it is almost a destination in itself.

5
The North

Most of the green expanse of the northern district of Singapore has been spared the intensive reclamation and industrialization to which the other regions have been subjected. Here the same rainforest still cloaks the landscape as it did when Raffles first came ashore. Small farms growing fruit and vegetables and rearing poultry occupy the northernmost region. The scenery is a dramatic change from the skyscrapers of the downtown area.

Kranji War Memorial *
This memorial in Woodlands Road is dedicated to the Allied troops who lost their lives defending Singapore against the Japanese during World War II. Set in beautifully manicured grounds, rows of graves stand in impeccable lines like soldiers on parade across the undulating landscape. The names of those who died are engraved on the memorial wall. If you wish to inspect the register of the dead, it is available from the custodian. At the bottom of the cemetery stand the tombs of the first two presidents of Singapore, Yusof bin Ishak and Dr Benjamin Sheares. The cemetery is open every day from 07:00 to 18:00.

Mandai Orchid Gardens **
This orchid-covered hill on Mandai Lake Road is the country's largest commercial garden, set up in 1950. A colourful display of a wide variety of orchids can be admired throughout the year. The water gardens blan-

> **DON'T MISS**
>
> *** The beautiful open-concept **Singapore Zoological Gardens**.
> *** Join the world's only **Night Safari** to see nocturnal animals at their most active.
> ** The exotic world of orchids at **Mandai Orchid Gardens**.
> ** The magnificent Buddhist temple of **Kong Meng San Phor Kark See**.

Opposite: *Rainforest trees still stand in the rural northern region.*

The Mandai Orchid Gardens are filled throughout the year with a profusion of beautiful hybrid orchids.

keted with water-lilies complete the effect of floral profusion. Visitors can purchase gift-wrapped orchids; incentive and convention groups can have new orchid hybrids named after them to commemorate their visit. Unless you are a true enthusiast and want to spend the whole day studying the varieties, it is convenient to visit this garden and Singapore Zoo, next door, on the same trip. The garden is open daily, 08:30 to 17:30.

Singapore Zoological Gardens ***

Located on Mandai Lake Road on the eastern flank of the Seletar Reservoir, no wildlife lover should miss a visit to this exceptional zoo. Inaugurated in 1973, it is set in a beautiful park of 90ha (220 acres) and designed in accordance with the 'open zoo' concept pioneered by Carl Hagenbeck at Hamburg Zoo. The animals are kept in recreations of their natural habitats in enclosures without obvious barriers or fences. The illusion of freedom is enhanced by the presence of cascading waters and moats blanketed in lush tropical plants across which visitors can view the animals in safety.

There are over 2000 animals of 240 species, housed in 70 exhibits. Forty of these species are classified as endangered under the Convention on International Trade in Endangered Species (CITES). The zoo runs successful

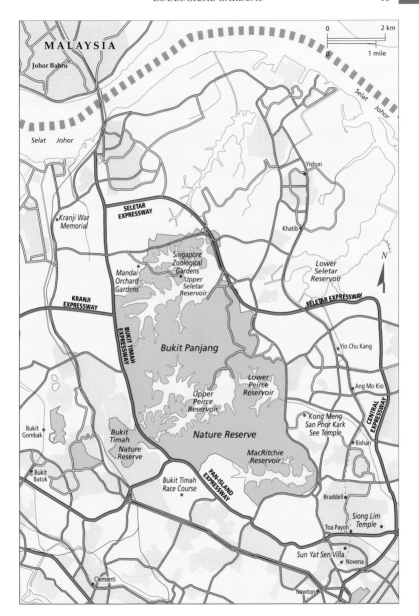

The world's heaviest lizard, the Komodo dragon, is found exclusively on the islands of Komodo, Rinca and Flores. Singapore Zoo boasts the only collection of these monsters outside Indonesia.

breeding programmes for some of these species: 16 orang-utans, one polar bear, one pygmy hippo, 11 rhinoceros iguanas and one ruffed lemur have been born in the zoo since 1973. It has the largest captive group of orang-utans in the world, numbering 25, and the only polar bears in the tropics! Don't miss the lion-viewing gallery, where the kings of the jungle are only a breath away from the visitors, separated by a sheet of toughened glass: you can get close enough to count their whiskers!

Educational animal shows, including breakfast with the orang-utans, are among the zoo's many programmes, making it an enjoyable and entertaining outing. A regular tram service with a taped commentary provides an overview of the zoo, but you can only really appreciate this delightful menagerie on foot. The zoo is open from 08:30 to 18:00 daily.

Night Safari ★★★

The world's first and only Night Safari Park was opened in May 1994. Adjacent to the Zoo itself, the 40ha (100 acre) park is laid out in a natural setting of tropical rainforest on a hillside. The trees cleared during construction were replanted to preserve the environment. There are 1000 nocturnal creatures of about 100 different species living in spacious natural habitats under subtle moonglow lighting. A 45-minute tram journey with a running

---

THE MAGICAL TWILIGHT WORLD OF CATS

Some of the most fascinating animals to be seen on the Night Safari are the cats of Southeast Asia. The **fishing cat** scoops fish out of the water with the speed of lightning before pinning its catch down with its paw. It will not swim after its prey but prefers to keep its feet dry on the bank. The **leopard**, with its black rosettes over greyish, pale yellow or rich chestnut fur, is a handsome creature with glowing green eyes. In the wild it feeds at night on antelope, deer, monkeys, pigs and, when the opportunity arises, domestic livestock. The largest and most majestic of all cats is the highly endangered **tiger**, lord of the Asian forests. It is a nocturnal and solitary creature and a competent swimmer. An adult may measure over 2.5m (8ft) and weigh more than 200kg (450 lb).

commentary covers the highlights of the zoo, guiding you round various geographical regions: a Nepalese river valley, Equatorial Africa, the South American pampas, Asian riverine forest or a Burmese hillside.

Clearly marked trails are named after various animals, and following these you weave through the forest along the dimly lit paths. The animals are bathed in special lighting which does not disturb their nocturnal habits. The atmosphere is thrilling: the cacophony of the incessant song of the cicadas is punctuated by the calls of animals great and small in well-orchestrated animal magic. The indigenous animals of each region, kept safe without obvious barriers, carry on their nightly routines oblivious of the spectators.

In order not to startle or alarm the animals, silence should be observed and no flash photography is allowed, as constant exposure to the lights could blind these nocturnal creatures.

Bukit Timah Nature Reserve ★★

This rainforest reserve covering 81ha (200 acres) is one of only two of its kind in the world (the other being in Rio de Janeiro) in that it lies within the boundaries of a city. Visitors can hike through the jungle along well-marked trails which are best tackled in the cool morning air wearing sensible walking shoes. Those with keen eyes and ears will be rewarded by the sight of brilliant butterflies flitting among the thick foliage, exotic birds winging freely in the green canopy or inquisitive monkeys peering from the branches. Squirrels and lemurs are amongst the other wildlife found here. Unusual plants, such as the insect-eating pitcher plants, can be found here and there in the lush greenery. At the heart of the reserve rises **Bukit Timah**, the highest point in Singapore at a height of 165m (542ft). The reserve is open daily.

Kong Meng San Phor Kark See Temple ★★

Reputed to be the largest religious building in Singapore, this Buddhist temple at 88 Bright Hill Drive in the centre of the island is grandiose not just in size but in its lavish

BUKIT TURF CLUB

This famous race course, reputedly the best in the region, covers 140ha (350 acres) of hillocks and valleys. Two race tracks run 32 race days a year, commanding crowds of over 26,000 at each event. The prestigious Singapore Gold Cup is the main event in the racing calendar, followed by other races such as the Gold Cup, Singapore Derby, Lion City Cup, Raffles Cup, Queen Elizabeth II Cup and the Pesta Sukan Cup. Prize money ranges from S$150,000 to S$700,000. Apart from racing, the club has restaurants, a pub and food court, a jogging track, golf course and driving range, plus the first public riding school in Singapore. On non-racing days, turf events from Ipoh, Kuala Lumpur and Penang are telecast live on giant screens. Tours of the race course are available, including a buffet lunch and entrance to the members' enclosure.

decoration and architectural design. The complex spreads over 8ha (19 acres) and includes shrines, pagodas, pavilions, bridges and a crematorium, all weighed down with mythological figures of dragons, phoenix, figurines and flowers. A large pond in the garden brims with turtles which are released into it by devotees on special occasions to bring good luck.

The main hall of the Siong Lim Temple at Toa Payoh.

DR SUN YAT SEN

Dr Sun Yat Sen, the Chinese revolutionary, first came to Singapore in 1900 to rally support for his movement to transform the China of the Manchu Dynasty into a modern republic. With the help of businessmen in Singapore, he set up the Singapore branch of Tung-ming Hui, the Chinese Revolutionary League, the forerunner of the Kuomintang, in 1906. After a spell of initial disappointment and lack of support, he was hailed as a conquering hero by the Singapore Chinese after the successful Chinese uprising of Wu-ch'ang in 1911. Contributions from the Singapore Chinese played a major role in the eventual revolution in China which brought Sun Yat Sen to power.

Sun Yat Sen Villa *

During Sun Yat Sen's eight visits to Singapore, he stayed at the villa of one of his supporters, Teo Eng Hock, a wealthy businessman who had bought the house for his mother. The handsome, but not outstanding, villa stands on Tai Gin Road near Toa Payoh. It houses a collection of old photographs of events in China during Dr Sun's era and of Singapore during the war, and a collection of personal effects of victims of the Japanese. It is open from Monday to Friday, 09:00 to 17:00, Saturday 09:00 to 15:00.

Siong Lim Temple **

Located at 184E Toa Payoh in the central region of Singapore, this Buddhist temple was built in 1908 and is now gazetted as a national monument. It was founded by a Chinese abbot to commemorate the birth and death of Buddha, a dedication which gives rise to its name of 'Twin Groves of the Lotus Mountain'. An ornately decorated gateway reached across a bridge opens into a courtyard. The grand building is guarded against evil by the Four Kings of Heaven. There are several shrines dedicated to various deities, including the Goddess of Mercy and the Laughing Buddha: the latter's stomach is often rubbed by visitors who believe the gesture will bring them good luck.

Out of Town at a Glance

GETTING AROUND

All parts of the island are accessible by public transport from the city centre.

The South and West

Singapore Botanic Gardens
MRT to Orchard (N3), then SBS 7, 105, 106, 123 or 174 from Orchard Blvd.

Holland Village
MRT to Buona Vista (W7). From Orchard Blvd take SBS 7, 105 or 106.

Mount Faber
MRT to Redhill (W4) then SBS 145. If you wish to travel by taxi it is advisable to book a return trip as there is no taxi service here. Alternatively, you can join a local coach tour which includes transport and a guide.

Haw Par Villa
MRT to Clementi (W8) then SBS 10 or MRT to Buona Vista (W7) then SBS 200.

New Ming Village
MRT to Clementi (W8), then taxi or SBS 78.

Singapore Science Centre
MRT to Jurong East (W9), then SBS bus 335 or taxi.

Chinese and Japanese Gardens
5 min walk from MRT Chinese Garden (W10).

Tang Dynasty City
MRT to Lakeside (W11), then SBS 154 or 240 opposite the station.

Jurong Bird Park and Crocodile Paradise
MRT to Boon Lay (W12), then SBS 251, 253 or 255.

East Coast and Changi
Geylang and Katong
MRT to Payar Lebar (E5); short taxi ride to Katong. From Orchard Rd, SBS 14 or 16 to Katong.

Singapore Crocodilarium
MRT Payar Lebar (E5) or Eunos, then taxi.

Air Force Museum and Changi Prison and Village
MRT to Tanah Merah (E9), then SBS 2 (or 9 for Air Force Museum).

The North

Kranji War Memorial
TIBS 182 from Hill St, or taxi.

Mandai Orchid Gardens and Singapore Zoo
MRT to Yishun (N12) then SBS 171, or MRT to Yio Chu Kang (N10) and SBS 138. A Zoo Express coach service operates from most major hotels: call 2353111 or 7322123 for pick-up (there is a charge for this service).

Bukit Timah Nature Reserve
MRT to Newton (N4) then SBS 67, 170, 171 or TIBS 182.

Kong Meng San Phor Kark See
Taxi from MRT Bishan (N8)

Sun Yat Sen Villa and Siong Lim Temple
MRT to Toa Payoh (N6).

WHERE TO EAT

The South and West
Alkaff Mansion, 10 Telok Blangah Green (Mt Faber), tel 278 6979. Indonesian buffet or western (mainly French) cuisine.

Klongtan Ping, Lorong Mambong, Holland Village. Thai Teochew restaurant.

Ponggol Seafood Restaurant, World Trade Centre.

Raffles Marina Yacht Club, 10 Tuas West, tel 861 8000. The restaurant serves both western and local food. Open to non-members on weekdays only.

The North
Ramu's Curry, Thomson Rd. Southern Indian cuisine.

Farrer's Xiang Ji Eating House, Farrer Road.

The East
The area is famous for its seafood restaurants.

Golden Lagoon Seafood, Blk 1206, East Coast Parkway.

Ponggol Seafood, 1110 East Coast Parkway.

Seafood Palace, East Coast Recreation Centre, 1000 East Coast Parkway.

Geylang Serai Food Centre, Geylang Serai.

TOURS AND EXCURSIONS

Numerous sightseeing and special interest tours are available, and can be booked through your hotel or with one of the companies listed on page 73. Here are a few suggestions:

Round island tours.

Night Safari (3-hr tour including a tram ride).

Singapore by Night.

Helicopter Sightseeing Tour.

Shop till you Drop Tour (visits places off the usual tourist circuit such as Toa Payoh shopping centre and Tse Sui Luen jewellery factory).

6
The Islands of Singapore

Singapore itself may not have an idyllic beachfront to boast about, but some of its 58 neighbouring islands are worth visiting if you want a day away from it all. Singaporeans suffering from city fatigue flock to the islands for weekend getaways to 'detoxify'. **Sentosa** dominates the water just off the southern tip of Singapore, with **Kusu**, **St John's**, **Pulau Hantu**, **Pulau Seking**, **Lazarus** and **Sisters Islands** clustering nearby. In the north **Pulau Ubin** lies just off the eastern shore of Singapore in the Straits of Johor, bordering mainland Malaysia.

In ancient times the waters around Singapore were treacherous highways, full of marauding pirates preying on passing ships. Even as early as the 13th century, Arab traders spoke of islands from which 'armed black pirates with poisoned arrows emerge'. In the 18th century, sea nomads known as Orang Selat, or 'straits people', lay in wait around Singapore. The notorious Orang Gallang from the neighbouring Riau Archipelago organized themselves into 'pirate armadas', led by Malay *prahus* or war-boats, while the meeker Orang Gelam from the same area restricted their piractical activities to pillaging stranded and helpless boats and killing their crews. The much feared and dangerous Sulu pirates and the Illanun from Mindanao ruled the sea in their heavily armed boats.

Piracy brought trade almost to a standstill until eventually in 1835 the British government in India took action to keep the pirates in check for a while. But in the early

DON'T MISS

On Sentosa:
*** A 'walk in the sea' in **Underwater World**.
*** **Fort Siloso**'s war-time tableaux.
*** A glimpse of old Singapore at the **Pioneers of Singapore and Surrender Chambers** museum.
Plus:
** The legendary island of **Kusu** and the historic **St John's.**
** The rustic atmosphere of **Pulau Ubin,** with its excellent seafood restaurant.

Opposite: *Sentosa ferry terminal offers a dazzling welcome to evening visitors.*

Sentosa is easily accessible by ferry, but is more excitingly reached by cable car from Mount Faber or the World Trade Centre, offering a bird's-eye view of the harbour.

1850s, Chinese pirates became active and openly used Singapore to trade in arms and to sell their loot. It was not until the late 1800s that treaties were signed between the western powers and China to eradicate piracy. The emergence of Dutch power in Sumatra and the extended protection of the British over the Malay states also contributed to its suppression. Captured pirates were sent to Calcutta for trial, but many ships' captains meted out their own justice by throwing the pirates overboard *en route* to India.

SENTOSA ISLAND
Promoted as Singapore's 'Discovery Island', the attractions here are entirely man-made, elaborately planned by the Sentosa Development Corporation for the 'enjoyment and recreation of Singaporeans and tourists'. Lying just half a kilometre from mainland Singapore and linked to it by a causeway, Sentosa is 3km (2 miles) in length and 1km (half a mile) wide. This island was once called Pulau Blakang Mati, the 'Island of Death Behind', a name derived from its savage past when Bugis pirates used to plunder and loot the settlement, leaving dead bodies behind. During World War II the British used it as a military base. It has since then been renamed Sentosa, which means 'tranquillity' in Malay, and transformed into a

modern resort with undeniably superb amenities. The attractions are based on themes of nature, history and fantasy.

Asian Village **

This village is a showcase for the music, ethnic food, arts, crafts and architecture of the various countries of Asia. There are regular cultural shows drawn from the diverse heritage of the continent. Visitors can sample the indigenous cuisines of the different regions in the food centre, food court and various restaurants. For children, the **Family Entertainment Centre** offers 11 exciting rides. The village is open every day from 10:00 to 21:00, with shows at 11:00 and 15:30.

Underwater World ***

Asia's largest tropical oceanarium houses over 2000 species of fish kept in a series of aquaria including a giant acrylic funnel rising from the floor in which visi-

> ### SINGAPORE'S VERY OWN VOLCANO
>
> An eruption on Sentosa Island, just before the Lunar New Year in January 1995, filled the air with ash and smoke and the stench of sulphur. But those watching, instead of fleeing for their lives, revelled in the spectacle. This was no real volcano but the centrepiece of Singapore's latest theme park, the S$20 million VolcanoLand.

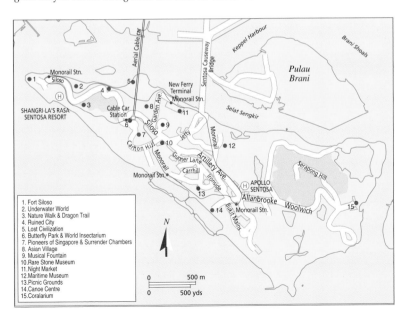

1. Fort Siloso
2. Underwater World
3. Nature Walk & Dragon Trail
4. Ruined City
5. Lost Civilization
6. Butterfly Park & World Insectarium
7. Pioneers of Singapore & Surrender Chambers
8. Asian Village
9. Musical Fountain
10. Rare Stone Museum
11. Night Market
12. Maritime Museum
13. Picnic Grounds
14. Canoe Centre
15. Coralarium

Defence posts from World War II still stand on Sentosa, relics of the British forces' mistaken belief that a Japanese attack would come from the sea.

tors can view the fish from all angles. The highlight of the attraction is the 90m (100yd) submerged acrylic tunnel which allows visitors to travel under the water on a moving walkway to view the marine life. It is a fantastic aquatic experience to be surrounded by menacing sharks, leered at by moray eels lurking in the rocks and swept over by sting-rays without even getting wet. Divers can sometimes be seen swimming among the fish offering them morsels of food. A marine theatre projects a continuous educational film on the conservation of sea life. The oceanarium is open from 09:00 to 21:00 daily.

Fort Siloso ★★★

Situated at the western tip of the island, this 19th-century British fort was the last bastion of the British forces during the Japanese invasion of Singapore in 1942. It is a maze of look-out points, giant cannons and underground tunnels filled with the re-created sounds of battle. Wax tableaux in the barrack-rooms depict a typical officer's quarters, complete with a nodding greyhound and photographs of the soldier's loved ones; the fort's laundry-room is staffed by a Chinaman, while a Chinese tailor measures an officer for his new uniform. All these scenes are animated, with atmospheric sound effects and snippets of conversation. An air-conditioned mini-theatre

---

THE GUARDIANS OF VOLCANOLAND

Towering over Sentosa's new 'volcano' is an ancient *Jelutong* tree which was spared because a pair of hornbills were found to be nesting in it. The birds stayed on, unperturbed by the building work, though the male was taken ill after pecking at pieces of rubber on the construction site and a vet had to be summoned to cure the ailing bird: he made a full recovery. Every evening they would fly off on their nocturnal routine leaving the tree free for cockatoos to roost, returning at dawn to reclaim their nesting-place.

shows a short film about the war at frequent intervals. Opening time: 09:00 to 19:00 daily.

Butterfly Park and Insect Kingdom Museum **

A colourful collection of 2500 butterflies of over 50 species fly freely in the butterfly garden. The Insect Kingdom Museum houses specimens of strange-looking insects like three-horned beetles, which resemble an armoured tank, hairy tarantulas and a host of other creepy-crawlies. Both collections are open from 09:00 to 18:00 Monday to Saturday and from 09:00 to 18:30 on Sunday and public holidays.

Pioneers of Singapore and Surrender Chambers ***

This fascinating museum charts the history of Singapore from the 14th century up to the surrender of the Japanese Army in 1945. Tableaux featuring life-size wax figures depict various historical events that shaped Singapore, with realistic animations complete with sound effects. There are interesting reconstructions of the lifestyle of early settlers, including one which shows the typical living quarters of Chinese coolies in the 19th century, in which an opium smoker is sprawled on a wooden bunk while a pot of rice is boiling over on the hot stove in the corner. You can witness the signing of the formal treaty between Raffles and the local rulers when he arrived to set up the trading post in 1819. There are various film clips from World War II and the exhibition ends on a sombre note with the surrender of the Japanese to Lord Louis Mountbatten, then British Supreme Allied Commander, in 1945, with all the key figures present. Opening times are 09:00 to 21:00 daily.

Coralarium/Nature Ramble *

At the eastern end of the island, accessible by bus, the Coralarium houses a small exhibition of living corals displayed in glass tanks. There is also a display of shells from all over the world. A nature park is set up in the grounds. Don't miss the **Touch Pool** where you can handle harmless live sea creatures including – if you wish –

PLANNING YOUR VISIT

It would be a feat of endurance to try to see everything on Sentosa in one trip. To help you decide which of the island's numerous attractions to visit, take a ride on the monorail which circles the island. A running commentary points out the various features on the route.

Many of Sentosa's numerous attractions are linked by monorail so that you can get an overview of the island before deciding what to see first.

Sentosa's beaches offer a chance to relax after a rigorous day's sightseeing.

the slimy giant sea cucumber (which is a great delicacy among the Chinese). On your nature walk you will have close encounters with macaques waiting for an opportunity to snatch food or drinks, cockerels and hens scratching for worms and peacocks in full regalia screeching for attention. Opening time is 09:00 to 19:00 daily.

Sun World ★★

After a day of zooming around the various attractions, Sun World is a good place to relax and recover from sightseeing fatigue. The man-made beach is ideal for sunbathing and the lagoons offer a tempting dip in the sea (if you remembered to pack your swimwear). Aquabiking, canoeing and windsurfing are all on offer. For keen golfers there are challenging golf courses nearby.

Museum of Rare Stones ★

An exhibition of semi-precious and rare stones, including fossils, collected in China over five generations by the family who owns the collection. Opening time: 09:00 to 19:00 daily.

The Musical Fountains ★★

The fountains near the ferry terminal liven up at night with a spectacle of water formations bathed in coloured lights and synchronized with classical and contemporary music. Shows start at 19:30, 20:00, 20:30 and 21:00.

Orchid Fantasy ★★

Horticultural enthusiasts will enjoy Orchid Fantasy, where orchids galore are planted in manicured gardens enhanced by a Japanese tea-house. Other attractions include an orchid flower clock, an 80-year-old 'Bell of Happiness' and a pond containing rare Japanese carp. The garden is open daily from 09:30 to 18:30.

A TRIP ON A TONGKANG

If you are seeking a tour with a real flavour of the East, you could take a trip to the southern islands aboard a restored *tongkang*, or Chinese junk. Although these days the old wooden boats are powered by engines, their sloping decks and strings of Chinese lanterns convey a sense of their colourful past as you gaze out at the view over the rail of the open-sided cabin. Two companies operate the junks, and as well as daytime cruises the boats set out at sunset for a tour which includes dinner on board.

The Islands of Singapore at a Glance

Sentosa

Sentosa is open daily; you should allow a full day to enjoy the major attractions (and don't forget to pack your swimming gear if you want to spend some time on the beach). There is a basic entrance fee, exclusive of transportation onto the island but inclusive of all internal transportation and a one-way bus journey out of the resort to designated destinations in mainland Singapore.
Special Sentosa Bus Services: From Orchard Rd take Orchard service E; from Tiong Bahru MRT take service B or C (note: service B operates only on Sat, Sun, public holidays and school holidays); from World Trade Centre bus terminal take service A. All bus fares include return trip on the bus, entrance fee and all internal transportation. There are also SBS bus services from Orchard Rd (65 and 145) and from Chinatown (61, 84, 143, 145, 166) to World Trade Centre (from there take Sentosa service A). Ferries operate from World Trade Centre, 10:00 to 21:00 daily, and the cable car runs from Mount Faber, 08:00 to 21:00 daily.

Kusu and St John's

Regular ferry services operate from the World Trade Centre to the two islands, calling at Kusu first, then St John's. Ferry departs at 10:00 and 13:30 (Mon–Sat),

09:45–17:00 every 90 mins (Sun and public holidays). Journey time is 30 mins to Kusu, 1 hr to St John's.

Pulau Hantu, Pulau Seking, Lazarus and Sisters Islands

There are no regular ferry services but bumboats can be hired from Jardine Steps at the World Trade Centre or Clifford Pier with a minimum of 10–15 passengers.

Pulau Ubin

Take MRT to Tanah Merah (E9), then SBS bus 2 to Changi Point. It is a short walk to Changi Jetty, where bumboats can be hired for the 10-min trip. There is no regular ferry service.

Sentosa

There is a continuous monorail service linking all the main attractions as well as bus services or trolley cars operating to areas of the island not covered by the monorail. Bicycles can be hired from the kiosk by the ferry terminal at an hourly rate (the best way to see the island independently). Taxis are not available on Sentosa.

Pulau Ubin

Mountain bikes are available for hire in the village.

Sentosa

Luxury

Shangri-la's Rasa Sentosa Resort, 101 Siloso Rd, tel 275 0100, fax 275 0355. Chinese restaurant, swimming pool,

sports facilities, business and convention centres.
The Beaufort Singapore, Bukit Manis Rd, tel 275 0331, fax 275 0228. Restaurants serving local and international cuisine, swimming pool, tennis and squash courts, health facilities, function rooms and convention facilities.
Budget
There is a Youth Hostel and a campsite near Central Beach.

Sentosa

Apart from food outlets at some of the attractions, such as **Asian Village** and **Underwater World**, the **Rasa Sentosa** food centre near the ferry terminal and at the hotels, there is a Mississippi-style riverboat restaurant which serves Chinese cuisine on the upper deck and fast food on the lower deck, while the bridge deck offers a scenic view of the Singapore skyline.

Pulau Ubin

Ubin Seafood, tel 5458202, is popular with Singaporeans.

Sentosa

To join an organized tour, contact one of the following companies:
RMG Tours Pte, 109C Amoy St, tel 220 8722, fax 222 5339.
Holiday Tours and Travel, 300 Orchard Rd, The Promenade, tel 738 2622, fax 733 3226.

7
Excursions from Singapore

Singapore is pivotally placed for excursions to its neighbouring countries: across the causeway to mainland Malaysia and over the sea to Indonesia. A short flight or a quick boat trip will whisk you to island resorts like the legendary shores of **Pulau Tioman**, the ultra-chic **Pangkor Laut Resort** or to **Johor**, the 'backyard' of Singapore. An elegant train journey on the **Eastern and Oriental train** will take you in style to **Kuala Lumpur**, capital of Malaysia. The islands of **Batam** and **Bintan** in the Riau Archipelago in Indonesia offer tempting rustic scenery as well as sea and sand.

Johor *

Linked by a 1km (half mile) causeway to Singapore, Johor, the southernmost state in Peninsular Malaysia, has always been the favourite playground of Singaporeans. Every weekend the causeway is congested with traffic from Singapore as the crowd heaves its way across to patronize the many inexpensive (compared with Singapore) seafood restaurants in Johor Bahru or Kukup while others head for the beach in Desaru. It is said that Singaporeans come here to let their hair down away from their restrictive existence at home.

Johor Bahru, the capital of Johor, is a bustling town where modernity mingles with the colonial past and quaint Malay villages. Its appeal lies in the many shopping complexes, seafood restaurants and grand buildings of a bygone era. Time permitting, places worth visiting are the **Istana Besar** (Grand Palace) the **Royal Abu**

Pangkor Laut

MALAYSIA

Kuala Lumpur • Tioman

• Melaka

Johor Bahru •
SINGAPORE

INDONESIA
Batam Bintan

DON'T MISS

*** A journey in style aboard the **E & O Express** into Malaysia.
*** The bustling and exciting city of **Kuala Lumpur**.
*** The exclusive resort of **Pulau Pangkor Laut**.
*** The resplendent beauty of legendary **Pulau Tioman**.
*** The rich cultural heritage of **Melaka**, ancient capital of the Malay Sultanate.

Opposite: *Domes and minarets crown the Masjid Jamek in downtown Kuala Lumpur.*

Bakar Museum and the **Istana Bukit Serene**, the official residence of the present sultan (only the garden is open to the public). The **Sultan Abu Bakar Mosque** is nearby.

Venturing southwest out of Johor Bahru through pineapple and palm oil plantations, you come to **Kukup**, a fishing village raised on stilts. Here the seafood restaurants are renowned for their prawn and chilli crab dishes. It is for these mouth-watering culinary delights that tourists on package tours and Singaporeans flock here, especially at weekends. On the northeast coast lies **Desaru**, the mainland beach resort of Johor (it is also blessed with a marine park of seven islands with excellent beaches just off the coast). Desaru's 20km (13 miles) of sandy beaches are not as tempting as further up the coast in Pahang; nevertheless they offer a convenient respite from the rat race of city life for Singaporeans. Desaru is 88km (55 miles) from Johor Bahru and is accessible by car, bus or ferry from Singapore.

Melaka's historic colonial buildings include the Stadthuys of 1650 and Christ Church of 1753.

Melaka **

The historic town of Melaka was founded by Parameswara, a refugee Sumatran prince, in the late 14th century. It became the centre of the Malay Sultanate during the 15th century. Its importance as a trading post, notably in the spice trade, brought it to the attention of the Portuguese, who conquered the port in 1511. The **Porta de Santiago**, the gateway which is all that remains of the huge fortress of **A Famosa**, is now the only concrete legacy of Portuguese rule. However, a small community of Eurasians, the product of intermarriage between the locals and their colonial rulers, still thrives today, keeping alive Portuguese traditions and speaking Cristao, a 16th-century dialect which is rarely spoken in present-day Portugal. The Dutch defeated the Portuguese in 1641 and colonized Melaka until it was handed over to the British in 1824 in exchange for Bencoolen in West Sumatra.

The influence of its European rulers over the centuries, in addition to the Peranakan and indigenous Malay cultures, have given this old town a cultural richness which makes it a worthwhile destination for an excursion from Singapore. Its famous Peranakan (Nonya) cuisine, a blend of Malay and Chinese culinary styles, is a must for food lovers. The heritage trail around old Peranakan shophouses, antique shops and Chinese temples, and early colonial buildings such as the ruined **St Paul's Church**, the Dutch **Stadthuys** of 1650 (now the museum) and the 18th-century **Christ Church** will keep visitors enthralled for many hours. To appreciate Melaka (and its restaurants) fully it is worth staying for a night or two.

Eastern and Oriental (E & O) Express to Kuala Lumpur ★★★

A grand way to visit the capital of Malaysia is to travel in style on the Eastern and Oriental Express. Inaugurated in September 1993, it is the first train ever to transport passengers direct from Singapore and Kuala Lumpur to Bangkok without the need to change trains *en route*. The luxury train induces a feeling of nostalgia for the grand old colonial days of comfortable rattan chairs on the verandah, fine dining and tea dances with gentlemen in linen suits and ladies in elegant frocks. Today's passengers are those who wish to rekindle the romance of travelling in elegance and style. They also need to be in possession of a healthy bank account: such luxury does not come cheap. Accommodation comes in three categories. Top of the range are the presidential suites, which have two single beds, separate dressing rooms, a CD player and complimentary bar; next are the state compartments with two single beds; the sleeper compartments with

---

MAKING TRACKS ON THE PENINSULA

Railways came to Southeast Asia in the latter half of the 19th century, and opened up vast areas of land previously only accessible by boat or along jungle paths. Settlement and agriculture followed the spread of the network. The first railway in Malaya was built by the Sultan of Johor, but it was made of wood and was soon destroyed by ants. The first successful line opened in 1885. By 1909 the Federated Malay States Railway was operating between Kuala Lumpur and Penang, Seremban and Johor, reaching almost to the tip of the Peninsula. The growing importance of rail transportation was demonstrated in 1911 by the construction of Kuala Lumpur's palatial railway station and administration building.

The style and elegance of a bygone age of travel are recreated in the panelled dining saloon of the E & O Express.

upper and lower berths make up the third category. All beds convert to seats during the day. Each sleeping carriage has its own uniformed cabin steward who is on call for room service at all times. Tea and dinner are included in the fare.

Kuala Lumpur ★★★

The vibrant capital of Malaysia warrants more than a day trip, though it is possible to cover the main sights in a day. Kuala Lumpur, or KL as it is known locally, is a city of contrasts where modern skyscrapers jostle with grand colonial buildings, with old shophouses sandwiched in between them. **Merdeka Square** in the city centre is a good starting point for your tour. The square, which commemorates the country's independence in 1957, was in colonial days the city's sports ground for cricket, hockey, tennis and rugby matches. From here, the main places of interest, such as the handsome **Sultan Abdul Samad Building**, **St Mary's Church**, **Masjid Jamek** at the birthplace of KL at the confluence of the Gombak and Klang Rivers, and **Infokraf**, the craft centre, are all within walking distance.

Further afield across the Klang River is the **Central Market (Pasar Seni)**, an Aladdin's cave of shops and stalls selling arts, crafts, food and artefacts from Malaysia and its neighbouring countries. Nearby in Jalan Petaling is **Chinatown**, a hive of busy market stalls selling fake designer goods, clothes, electronic equipment and other consumer goods at bargain prices. The old shophouses which flank the street markets are showcases of the age-old lifestyle of the Chinese community, with traditional medicine shops, coffee shops, ironmon-

---

A CITY ON TWO RIVERS

The name 'Kuala Lumpur' means muddy rivermouth, and the city stands at the confluence of two rivers, the Klang and the Gombak. It began life inauspiciously as a small tin-mining community riddled with malaria which carried off almost the whole population in the first few weeks of its establishment. But the toughest of the prospectors survived and prospered, and within 40 years the little town had become the state capital of Selangor.

gers and goldsmiths. The groceries offer curious-looking edibles like wind-dried ducks (which look as if they have been flattened by a steamroller), dried mushrooms and gnarled sea cucumbers, while sweet-flavoured Chinese sausages hang in festoons from hooks in the five-foot way.

Outside the city centre, the **Lake Gardens**, the green lung of the city, comprise 92ha (230 acres) of beautiful lush vegetation, with an **Orchid Garden**, **Bird Park** and a **Butterfly Park**. The **National Museum**, in close proximity to the Lake Gardens, is worth a visit. It has extensive exhibitions of arts and crafts, local history, native flora and fauna, weapons and currency, in addition to a display of vintage forms of transport in the grounds.

272 Steps to the Gods

A mere 45-minute drive north from KL lie the famous Batu Caves. The massive limestone cavern was transformed into a Hindu temple in 1891. A climb of 272 steps, first passing over a small flame to symbolize spiritual cleansing, will take you to the abode of the gods. Devotees throng to the caves daily to pray and leave offerings, but the sombre air of the temple is enlivened by a menagerie of cats, monkeys, turkeys, chickens and pigeons, roaming freely and hoping that the visitors will feed them.

At the foot of the steps, fortune-tellers with stalls of mystical paraphernalia will read your palm or instruct their assistant (a parakeet or canary) to pick a card containing your future. The extent of their revelations will depend on the fee you are willing to part with.

Kuala Lumpur's Moorish-style Sultan Abdul Samad Building, erected in 1897.

KL is renowned for its shopping, and goods here can be better bargains than in Singapore. Silk, batik, oriental treasures, clothing, accessories and electronic goods are among the best buys here. The main shopping centres are dotted around the streets of the **Golden Triangle**: **Jalan Bukit Bintang**, **Jalan Sultan Ismail** and **Jalan Imbi**. There are other large departmental stores at **Jalan Ampang** and **Jalan Tun Razak**, while along **Jalan Tuanku Abdul Rahman** more traditional shophouses offer an array of goods.

Pulau Pangkor Laut ***

This little island lying off the coast of Perak is one of the most exclusive resorts in Malaysia. With a total area of 120ha (300 acres), this private island is run as the **Pangkor Laut Resort**, with villa-style accommodation centred on **Royal Bay**, the main beach front, and **Coral Bay** in the next cove. The well-appointed villas are luxuriously furnished and are fashioned in the style of traditional Malay houses built on stilts, some over the sea while others perch dramatically on the cliff face.

The jungle-clad interior harbours bountiful wildlife such as hornbills and other birds nesting in the green canopy of the rainforest, while long-tailed macaques eye visitors with mischievous intent. Pangkor Laut is blessed with beautiful sandy beaches, notably **Emerald Bay** on the other side of the island away from the villas, which has been voted one of the best 100 beaches in the world. White powdery sand sweeps round the bay, lapped by the emerald green waters from which the bay justly acquired its name.

A villa overlooking Royal Bay on the luxurious island resort of Pulau Pangkor Laut.

Clear blue water laps the golden beaches of beautiful Pulau Tioman, one of the world's loveliest islands.

Pulau Tioman ★★★

This island, measuring only 39km (25 miles) long and 19km (12 miles) wide, is endowed with great natural beauty and was chosen as the location for 'Bali Hai' in the film version of *South Pacific* in the 1950s. Its rugged forested terrain is fringed with golden sands bathed by warm clear waters of aquamarine. Tioman is a favourite with scuba divers and snorkellers, as the rich coral reef harbours some of the most diverse marine life in Malaysia, notably in the water off **Salang Beach**. The island is dominated by the luxurious **Berjaya Tioman Beach Resort**, the only international standard hotel here. There is plenty of more modest accommodation in chalets, A-frame huts and beach bungalows. Malay villages dotted around the island can be reached along jungle paths or by sea buses which transport visitors around the island.

THE INDONESIAN ISLANDS

Scattered across the South China Sea southeast of Singapore is a cluster of some 3000 Indonesian islands known as the **Riau Archipelago**. The two largest islands in the group, **Bintan** and **Batam**, have always been an irresistible lure for visitors from Singapore.

ISLAND OF LEGEND

Pulau Tioman, with its jungle-clad interior, mysterious peaks and golden coastline, is the stuff of which legends are made. It is said that the island was transformed from a dragon whose feet got stuck in the coral of the surrounding sea. The horns of the beast are manifest today as the famous twin peaks, Bukit Nenek Simukut and Bukit Batu Sirau, which rise out of the green canopy of the forest.

Bintan **

Bintan, the largest of the islands, lies 45km (28 miles) southeast of Singapore, off the eastern coast of Sumatra. Its population of 400,000 includes Malays, Bugis, Orang Laut (sea gypsies), Chinese, Arabs and Indians. Steeped in history and culture, Bintan is relatively undeveloped and is reminiscent of Singapore in the early 1960s. Most of the population is concentrated in **Tanjung Pinang**, the quaint main town, to the south of the island. It has a bustling port strategically located on major sea routes linking Singapore, Sumatra, Java, Madura and Sulawesi. Water taxis, known as *pompong*, can be hired to travel round the coast of Bintan or to visit neighbouring islands. **Senggarang**, a rustic fishing village just north of Tanjung Pinang, has a large population of Teochew Chinese whose ancestors settled here in the 18th century. They live in **Kampong Cina** (Chinese Village) in stilted houses perched over the sea.

Bintan's main attraction for visitors lies in its long stretch of palm-fringed sandy beaches on the northern coast, accessible from the south only along dirt tracks or by boat. This area has been earmarked to be Indonesia's next up-and-coming tourist destination. Under the auspices of Bintan Resort Management, a master plan for this tourism project has been devised as part of a 1990 joint economic agreement between the governments of Indonesia and Singapore to develop the Riau Province. Resort hotels, golf courses, marinas, amusement parks and street bazaars are on its agenda.

The Mayang Sari Beach Resort, with 100 beach chalets, targeted at the mid-range market, offers cosy accommodation. All rooms are comfortably furnished with air-conditioning. There is a coffee house with indoor and outdoor dining areas. Next to the resort is the Mana Mana Beach Club, a watersports centre which provides windsurfing, scuba diving, snorkelling, sailing, waterskiing and jetskiing. There is no accommodation here but there are restaurants, bars and a pro-shop. The newly-opened Banyan Tree Bintan is a luxury resort with villas perched high on a cliff commanding a spectacular

The palm-fringed beach of Pasir Panjang – which means 'long sands' – runs all along the north coast of Bintan in the Riau Archipelago.

view of the sea, a poolside restaurant and bar. An 18-hole golf course, swimming-pool, tennis court and watersports are available to guests. For dining, the Kelong Restaurant, built on stilts stretching 200m (650ft) out into the sea, serves fresh seafood caught before your very eyes. Live fish and shellfish are kept in netted pontoons accessed by walkways and are fished out as they are chosen from the menu.

Batam Island *

This duty free island is largely undeveloped, with rustic Malay villages hugging the sea edge while pockets of settlement are scattered on the island. Nagoya, the main town, has an unexciting assortment of hotels and shops. The seafood restaurants, built in *kelong* style above the sea, serve good sea fare and it is mainly for these that Singaporeans and Indonesian tourists come here. There are several hotels on the island to cater for the tourists. Two of its major resorts are the **Batam View Beach Resort** and the **Turi Beach Resort**. Batam View nestles on a peninsula surrounded by turquoise water. It offers various watersports, a 36-hole golf course and a seafood restaurant. The Balinese-style Turi Beach Resort has all the amenities of an international hotel with a health club and watersports. There are regular Indonesian cultural shows as well as weekend seafood barbecues at the poolside.

BINTAN'S HISTORY

Bintan has always been the main gateway to the Riau Archipelago. After the foundation of Melaka in 1400, Bintan and the rest of the Riau islands came under the control of the Melaka Sultanate. When the Sultan of Melaka fled from the Portuguese in 1511 he set up his capital in Bintan after an initial settlement in Johor. From 1513 to 1526, and again from 1722 to 1819, Bintan was the seat of the Johor-Riau kingdom. The Anglo-Dutch Treaty of London in 1824 brought the Archipelago under Dutch control, and the Riau Sultanate was dissolved in 1911.

Excursions from Singapore at a Glance

From Nov–Mar Pulau Tioman, Batam and Bintan are subject to heavy rain during the NE monsoon. The west coast of Peninsular Malaysia is sheltered from the NE monsoon, but gets most rain between Apr–Sep.

Johor

By car or bus service operated by Singapore-Johor Bahru Express Snd Bhd, Ban San Terminal, junction of Queen St and Arab St, tel 292 8149, 06:30-00:00 every 7 mins (journey takes 40 mins). Ferry leaves Changi Point to Tanjung Belungkor in E Johor, gateway to Desaru, Mersing and E Coast Peninsular Malaysia. Contact: Ferrylink (S) Pte Ltd, tel 733 9866 for reservations.

Melaka

Bus services operated by Melaka-Singapore Express Sdn Bhd at Lavender St/Kallang Car Park, tel 293 5915, departing every hour from 08:00 to 11:00 and from 14:00 to 16:00. Journey takes 4^1/2 hours.

Kuala Lumpur

By car, rail (Singapore Station tel 222 5165), by air with Singapore or Malaysia Airlines, or bus: Kuala Lumpur–Singapore Express Sdn Bhd at Ban San Terminal, junction of Queen St and Arab St, tel 292 8254.

Pulau Pangkor Laut

Flights by Pelangi Air from Singapore to Pulau Pangkor, then a 15-min boat ride. Or by road 4 hours from Kuala Lumpur to Lumut on Perak coast, and 45-min ferry ride to Pangkor Laut Resort.

Pulau Tioman

By air with Pelangi or Silk Air from Singapore, or 4^1/2-hour ferry ride from World Trade Centre, daily except Wed (contact Resort Cruises (S) Pte Ltd, tel 278 4677).

Bintan Island

High speed catamaran, MV Indera Bupala from World Trade Centre to Bandar Bentan Telani ferry terminal in N Bintan, departs at 08:40 and 13:05, returns 11:30 and 17:40 (journey time 1 hour). Ferry to Tanjung Pinang in S Bintan leaves World Trade Centre at 10:10 and 15:00 (journey time 2^1/2 hours). Bintan can also be reached from Batam Island.

Batam Island

Daily ferry service from World Trade Centre, 08:00-19:99, half-hourly (journey 45 mins).

Melaka

Luxury
Renaissance, Jl Bendahara, tel (06) 248888, fax 249269.
Mid-range
Emperor, Jl Munshi Abdullah, tel (06) 240777, fax 238989.
City Bayview, Jl Bendahara, tel (06) 239888, fax 236699.

Kuala Lumpur

Luxury
Hotel Istana, 73 Jl Raja Chulan, tel (03) 241 9988.

Kuala Lumpur Hilton, Jl Sultan Ismail, tel (03) 248 2322.
Mid-range
Ming Court Hotel, Jl Ampang, tel (03) 261 8888
Swiss Garden Hotel, 117 Jl Pudu, tel (03) 241 3333
Plaza Hotel, Jl Raja Laut, tel (03) 298 2255.
Hotel Grand Continental, Jl Belia, tel (03) 292 9333.
Budget
Apollo Hotel, 106-110, Jl Bukit Bintang, tel (03) 242 8133.
Colonial Hotel, 29-45 Jl Sultan, tel (03) 238 0336.

Pulau Pangkor Laut

Pangkor Laut Resort, tel (05) 6851375, fax (05) 6851320.

Pulau Tioman

Luxury
Berjaya Tioman Beach Resort; sales office: PO Box 4, Mersing, Johor, tel (09) 445445, fax (09) 445718.
Mid-range – Budget
Nazri's Place, Kg Air Batang, tel (011) 349534.
Salang Indah, Kg Salang, tel (011) 730230.
Samudra Swiss Cottage, Kg Tekek, tel (07) 248728.
Tioman Paya Resort, Kg Paya; reservations (Mersing): tel (07) 792602/792169, fax (07) 792603.

Melaka

Restoran Peranakan Town House, 107 Jl Tun Tan Cheng Lock, cultural show nightly (except Saturdays).

Excursions from Singapore at a Glance

Ole Sayang Restaurant, 198 & 199 Taman Melaka Jaya.
My Baba's, 164 Jl Munshi Abdullah.
Gluttons' Corner at Jl Taman, Bandar Hilir: numerous stalls sell various Chinese, Malay and Indian dishes.

Kuala Lumpur
There are numerous inexpensive food courts in most shopping centres, notably Sungei Wang, Chinatown and Central Market. Bangsar, south of KL, is a trendy place to eat out, with hawker stalls and restaurants serving all cuisines. Hotel restaurants serve mostly Chinese or western food, while their coffee houses offer local as well as international fare.

Chinese
The Blossom Chinese Restaurant, Swiss Garden Hotel, Jl Pudu, tel (03) 241 3333.
Tsui Yuen Chinese Restaurant, Kuala Lumpur Hilton, Jl Sultan Ismail, tel (03) 248 2322.
Futt Yow Yuen (vegetarian), 9 Jl Balai Polis, tel (03) 238 5704.
Malay
Eden Village, 260 Jl Raja Chulan, tel (03) 241 4027: best known for seafood.
Nelayan Floating Restaurant, Titiwangsa Lake Gardens, tel: (03) 422 8600.
Seri Melayu, Jl Conlay (nr KL Hilton), tel (03) 245 1833.
Dondang Sayang Restoran, Ming Court Hotel, Jl Ampang, tel (03) 261 8888.

Indian
Taj Restaurant, Crown Princess Hotel, Jl Tun Razak, tel (03) 262 5522.
Bilal Restaurant, 33 Jl Ampang, tel (03) 238 0804.
Bangles Restaurant, 60-A Jl Tuanku Abdul Rahman, tel (03) 298 6770.
International
The Ship, 102-4 Jl Bukit Bintang, tel (03) 244 3605.
Coliseum Café, Jl Tuanku Abdul Rahman, tel (03) 292 6270. Famous for sizzling steaks cooked at the table.

TOURS AND EXCURSIONS

Johor
For organized tours contact: **RMG Tours**, tel 738 7776, fax 235 5256; **Holiday Tours**, tel 738 2622, fax 733 3226; **Gray Line Tours**, tel 331 8244, fax: 337 6056.

Melaka
For organized tours contact: **Holiday Tours**, as above; **Morning Star Travel**, tel 292 9009, fax 292 4340.

E & O Express
Train leaves from Singapore Keppel Road Station, journey takes $7^1/_2$ hours to Kuala Lumpur; at least two departures per week, depending on time of year. For further details contact E & O office (Singapore) tel 227 2068, fax 224 9265.

Kuala Lumpur
City sightseeing: day or evening tours last about 3 hours. Day trips to Batu Caves, batik and Royal Selangor Pewter factories and many others. Excursions can be booked through most hotels or tour companies:
Peter Stuyvesant Travel Service, The Weld, Lot 1.08, Jl Raja Chulan, tel (03) 262 0333.
Asia Overland, 33M, Jl Dewan Sultan Sulaiman, tel (03) 292 5622.

Bintan Island
For organized tour to Tanjung Pinang contact: **Rapid Travel**, tel 734 6147, fax 734 8531; **Nam Ho Travel**, tel 221 8433, fax 225 2588.

Batam Island
For organized tours contact: **RMG Tours**, as above; **Singapore Sightseeing Tour East**, tel 235 5703, fax 235 1075; **Holiday Tours**, as above.

USEFUL CONTACTS

World Trade Centre Ferry Terminal, tel 271 4866.
Malaysia Tourism Promotion Board (Tourism Malaysia), 17, 24th-27th Floor, Menara Dato' Onn, Putra World Trade Centre, 45 Jl Tun Dr Ismail, 50480 Kuala Lumpur, tel (03) 293 5188, fax (03) 293 5884.
Malaysia Tourist Information Centre (MATIC), 109 Jl Ampang, Kuala Lumpur, tel (03) 242 3929.
Bintan Resort Management Pte Ltd, 3 Lim Teck Kim Rd #10-01, Singapore Technologies Building, Singapore 0208, tel (65) 221 2328, fax (65) 225 1089.

Travel tips

Tourist Information

The Singapore Tourist Promotion Board has offices worldwide to provide general assistance and information on Singapore.

Head office: Raffles City Tower, #36-04, 250 North Bridge Road, Singapore 0617, tel 339 6622, fax 339 9423.

Information centres: Raffles City Shopping Centre #01-19, 250 North Bridge Road, Singapore 0617, tel 330 0431/2; Scotts Shopping Centre, #02-02/03 Scotts Road, Singapore 0922, tel 738 3778/9.

Other STPB offices: Bombay, Chicago, Frankfurt, Hong Kong, London, Los Angeles, New York, Osaka, Paris, Perth, Seoul, Shanghai, Sydney, Taipei, Tokyo, Toronto, Zurich.

Entry Formalities

All visitors entering Singapore must be in possession of a valid passport or an internationally recognized travel document.

Visa requirements:

1. Citizens of the following countries do not need visas for social visits: Australia, Bangladesh, Brunei, Canada, Hong Kong, Liechtenstein, Malaysia, Monaco, Netherlands, New Zealand, Sri Lanka, Switzerland, the United Kingdom and the USA; holders of diplomatic special or official passports of the Philippines and Thailand.

2. Citizens of the following countries do not need visas for stays of up to 3 months; visas are required for stays exceeding 3 months: Austria, Belgium, Denmark, Finland, France, Germany, Italy, Iceland, Luxembourg, Japan, Norway, South Korea, Spain and Sweden.

3. Visas are required for the following nationals: Afghanistan, Algeria, Cambodia, India, Iraq, Jordan, Laos, Lebanon, Libya, Pakistan, People's Republic of China, CIS (Russia), Syria, Tunisia, Vietnam, Yemen, Hong Kong Documents of Identity issued in Hong Kong, and stateless persons residing in these countries.

4. Passport holders of Russian Federation, People's Republic of China, Laos, Vietnam, Cambodia and Afghanistan may transit in Singapore for 36 hours without a visa, provided they hold confirmed onward/return airline tickets and onward facilities to their next destination.

5. No visas are required for any other nationalities not mentioned above for social visits not exceeding 14 days. Holders of Taiwan passports do not require visas as tourists but they must have visa cards, which can be obtained free of charge from any Singapore overseas mission, the airlines or shipping companies.

Note: As regulations change from time to time, international visitors should check with the nearest Singapore overseas mission before departure. The final decision concerning entry into the country, irrespective of whether the person has a visa or not, is at the discretion of the Immigration Officer at the point of entry.

Women in an advanced state of pregnancy (i.e. six months or more) intending to visit Singapore should make prior applications to the nearest Singapore overseas mission or the Immigration Department.

Singapore Immigration Department 95 South Bridge Road, #07-00 Pidemco Centre, Singapore 0105, tel 532 2877, fax 530 1840.

Health Requirements

No vaccinations are required for Singapore except cholera or yellow fever if you have come from or visited an endemic zone 6 days prior to arriving in the country.

TRAFFICKING, MANUFACTURING, IMPORTING AND EXPORTING OF ILLEGAL DRUGS SUCH AS OPIUM, HEROIN, CANNABIS, MORPHINE, COCAINE AND CANNABIS RESIN CARRY THE DEATH PENALTY

Customs Formalities

Dutiable goods

- Liquors including wine, beer, ale, stout and port.
- Tobacco, including cigarettes and cigars.
- Garments and clothing accessories.
- Leather handbags and wallets.
- Imitation jewellery.
- Chocolate and sugar confectionery.
- Pastries, biscuits and cakes.

Non-dutiable goods

- Electronic and electrical goods.
- Cosmetics.
- Cameras, clocks and watches.
- Jewellery, precious stones and precious metal.

- Footwear.
- Arts and crafts.
- Toys.

Duty-free concessions for visitors

The following dutiable items may be brought into the country duty-free for personal consumption only:

- Personal effects in reasonable quantities.
- Prepared food such as chocolates, biscuits, cakes etc not exceeding S$50.00 in value.
- Travellers above 18 years old, arriving from countries other than Malaysia and who are spending not less than 48 hours in Singapore are entitled to duty free allowance of 1 litre spirits, 1 litre wine and 1 litre beer, stout, ale or port.

Prohibited items

- Liquor, cigarettes and tobacco specially marked for export with the label 'Singapore Duty Not Paid' and cigarettes with the prefix 'E' are restricted to consumption outside Singapore. Re-importation is not permitted.
- Controlled drugs and psychotropic substances.
- Firecrackers.
- Pistol- or revolver-shaped cigarette lighters.
- Toy coins and toy currency notes.
- Unauthorized reproductions of copyright publications, video tapes or discs, records or cassettes.
- Endangered species of wildlife and their by-

products.
- Obscene articles and publications.
- Seditious and treasonable materials.
- Chewing gum.

For further clarification or information contact: The Customs Duty Officer, Duty Office Terminal 1, Singapore Changi Airport, Singapore 9181, tel 542 7058/545 9122, or The Customs Duty Officer, Duty Office Terminal 2, Singapore Changi Airport, Singapore 9181, tel 543 0755/543 0754.

Changi Airport

Airport tax: There is a S$15.00 Passenger Services Charge payable at the airport upon your departure. Coupons for the airport tax can be bought at most hotels, travel agencies and airline offices. The coupon must be attached to your airline ticket.

Baggage storage: Both terminals provide baggage storage services at their arrival and departure halls.

Free tour: Passengers with at least four hours' transit time at Changi Airport can take advantage of a two-hour free sightseeing tour of Singapore (The City Tour), courtesy of the Civil Aviation Authority of Singapore, Singapore Airlines and STPB. To register, go to the 'Free City Sightseeing' desk in the transit lounge and produce your boarding pass and passport. The guided tour gives you a glimpse of Singapore, passing through Chinatown, Little India, Lau Pa Sat Festival Market,

Merlion Park and the Colonial District. Passengers must return with the coach to Changi Airport. The tour leaves at 10:30, 14:30 and 16:30 every day.

Medical Facilities

Singapore's medical facilities rank amongst the finest in the world, with well-qualified doctors and dental surgeons. Pharmaceuticals are available from numerous outlets, including supermarkets, department stores, hotels and shopping centres. Registered pharmacists operate from 08:00 to 16:30.

Travellers with medicine which may only be obtained on prescription under Singapore law, especially sleeping pills, anti-depressants and stimulants, must be in possession of a prescription from a physician confirming that the medicine is to be used solely for the traveller's physical well-being.

Most hotels have their own doctor on call around the clock. Doctors are listed in the Yellow Pages of the Singapore phone book. Visitors could also consult doctors at the following hospitals:

Gleneagles Medical Centre, 6 Napier Road, Singapore 1025, tel 470 3415.

Mount Alvernia Hospital, 820 Thomson Road, Singapore 2057, tel 253 8023.

Mount Elizabeth Hospital, 3 Mount Elizabeth, Singapore 0922, tel 737 2666.

Singapore General

Hospital, Outram Road, Singapore 0316, tel 222 3322.

Thomson Medical Centre, 339 Thomson Road, Singapore 1130, tel 256 9494.

As private medical fees are high in Singapore, visitors should ensure they are adequately covered by travel insurance.

Money Matters

Money can be changed at banks, hotels (usually at less favourable rates) and licensed money changers at most shopping complexes. It is not advisable to change money with unlicensed money dealers.

Currency: There is no restriction on the import or export of currency into or from Singapore. The local currency is Singapore dollars (S$ or SID) and cents. Notes come in denominations of S$1 (being phased out), S$2, S$5, S$10, S$20, S$50, S$100, S$500, S$1000 and S$10,000. Coins come in denominations of 5, 10, 20 and 50 cents and S$1.

Banks: As one of the world's largest banking centres, there are nearly 60 international banks in Singapore. Official banking hours are Monday to Friday, 10:00 to 15:00, Saturday 09:30 to 13:00 (some banks are open until 15:00). OCBC Bank branches in Orchard Road, Serangoon Gardens, Bedok and Yishun NorthPoint open on Sunday, 11:00 to 16:00. Most banks handle travellers' cheques and change foreign currencies. However, some banks do not deal in foreign exchange on Saturday. Passports are required when cashing travellers' cheques. A nominal commission may be charged.

Credit cards: All major credit cards are accepted at shops, big hotels (most small tourist class hotels accept cash only), and restaurants. There should be no surcharge on any credit card transaction and should any shop insist on adding one, you are advised to complain to the respective credit card company: American Express, tel 1800 732 2244; Citibank Visa, tel 1800 225 5225; Diners Card, tel 1800 292 7566; Hong Kong Bank

CONVERSION CHART		
FROM	**TO**	**MULTIPLY BY**
Millimetres	inches	0.0394
Metres	yards	1.0936
Metres	feet	3.281
Kilometres	miles	0.6214
Hectares	acres	2.471
Litres	pints	1.760
Kilograms	pounds	2.205
Tonnes	tons	0.984
To convert Celsius to Fahrenheit: $x \times 9 \div 5 + 32$		

Visa/Master Card, tel 336 5277; Malayan Banking Visa, tel 532 2604; OCBC Master Card, tel 1800 538 0118; OUB Credit Card Centre, tel 1800 221 7888; Standard Chartered Visa, tel 1800 227 7662; OUB Card Centre, tel 1800 253 6888.

Tipping: Tipping is not encouraged in Singapore as most hotels and restaurants levy a 10% service charge and 3% Goods and Service Tax (GST) on customers' bills. It is prohibited at the airport. However, a gratuity may be paid to a service-provider at your discretion if you are particularly pleased with their service, but it is illegal for them to demand a tip.

Official Business Hours

Monday to Friday: 09:00 to 17:00; Saturday 09:00 to 13:00.

Public Holidays

1 January: New Year's Day
*February: Chinese New Year
*March: Hari Raya Puasa
*April: Good Friday
1 May: Labour Day
*May: Hari Raya Haji
*May: Vesak Day
9 August:National Day
*October: Deepavali
25 December: Christmas Day

*Dates vary.

Telephones

Local calls made from pay phones cost 10 cents for every three minutes, with a maximum duration of 9 minutes. International calls can be made from your hotel, Comcentre at Exeter Road, Telephone House in Hill Street, airport and post offices with major credit cards or phone cards (available in denominations of S$2, S$5, S$10, S$20 and S$50) which can be purchased at shops and post offices. All operators speak English.

At Changi Airport, local calls from designated telephones (usually red or maroon in colour) are free of charge: useful if you arrive with no small change, and good for chatting to friends and relatives while waiting for your flight!

Useful numbers:
Emergencies: police 999, ambulance/fire brigade 995; operator-assisted international calls: 104; International Direct Dialling (IDD) access code 005; directory enquiries: 103; time of day: 1711.

Time

Singapore is 8 hours ahead of Greenwich (Universal Standard) Time, seven hours ahead of Central European Winter Time, and 13 hours ahead of the USA's Eastern Standard Winter Time.

Weights and Measures

Singapore uses the metric system.

Water

It is perfectly safe to drink water straight from the tap in Singapore. However, bottled mineral waters are available from supermarkets and grocers.

Electricity

Singapore voltage is 220-240 volts AC, 50 cycles per second. Most hotels will provide transformers or adaptors for visitors with electrical appliances of different voltage.

Shopping

STPB publishes a shopping guide to Singapore and a booklet listing members of its Good Retailers Scheme, whose members are acknowledged to offer good service and fair prices. These publications are available at STPB's information centres at Raffles Hotel Arcade and Scotts Shopping Centre as well as from hotel information desks. Shops displaying the red Merlion symbol are approved by the Consumer Association of Singapore and by STPB. Retailers are encouraged to use price tags on all goods and to display a window sticker advising whether their prices are fixed or only recommended.

Always avoid touts offering free shopping tours, special discounts or pirated goods. If you encounter retailer malpractice, you can get full compensation through the Small Claims Tribunals. For more information contact the Consumer Association of Singapore, tel 270 5433.

Tax Refund for Visitors

Bona fide visitors to Singapore can apply for a refund of the Goods and Service Tax (GST) of 3% they pay on their purchases of S$500 or more, at shops displaying the 'Tax Refund' logo. Goods must be bought from one shop or branches of one retail chain and must be taken out of Singapore within 2 months of purchase. Completed GST claim forms, together with the items purchased, must be presented for inspection by Customs at Changi Airport on your departure. GST claim forms will only be supplied in the shops when you produce your passport to prove your tourist status.

For inspection of large items to be checked in, go to the GST Refund Inspection Counter next to Departure Entrance 1 in the public area of the airport before you check in your luggage. For smaller items go to the GST Refund Counter in the departure lounge after clearing immigration. Refunds in Singapore dollars will normally be paid within 12 weeks by the shop and will be sent to your address, or credited to your account depending on your method of payment. For further details of the scheme, contact STPB Information Centres.

Disabled Travellers

Singapore Access is a guide giving details and charts of easily accessible attractions, and outlining facilities for physically disabled travellers at public places and buildings. It can be obtained from: The Singapore Council of Social Services, 11 Penang Lane, Singapore 0923, tel 336 1544/331 5417.

What to wear

To stay comfortable in Singapore's year-round heat and humidity, light loose clothing in natural fibres – cotton or silk – is recommended, particularly for walking around the city. You may need something thicker, however, to cope with chilly air-conditioning indoors. An umbrella is an invaluable source of protection from both sun and the inevitable tropical showers. Smart casual clothes are acceptable for most occasions, including evenings, though a few establishments may have a more formal dress code (check beforehand if you are unsure).

Language

There are four official languages in Singapore: English, Malay, Tamil and Chinese. English is widely used in administration, commerce and everyday life. Street signs and maps are all in English and taxi drivers understand it quite well. The language used between Singaporeans of different races is 'Singlish', a blend of English with Chinese and Malay words woven into it. A few Malay or Indonesian phrases would be useful if you are planning an excursion outside Singapore.

Public Behaviour

You need to bear in mind Singapore's various laws concerning public conduct if you wish to avoid a fine for infringing one of them.
Jaywalking: Crossing a road within 50m of a designated

pedestrian crossing, bridge or underpass is an offence.
Littering: A first offence results in a large fine; a subsequent offence means an even larger one and possibly some community service cleaning public places.
Smoking: Smoking is banned on public transport, in museums, libraries, lifts, theatres and cinemas, hair salons, shops and government offices. Many non-government offices are also non-smoking areas. It is an offence to smoke in air-conditioned restaurants.
Fines may also be imposed on anyone caught spitting in public places, failing to flush a public toilet, or carrying durians or fast food on the MRT or into public buildings. Chewing gum is not in itself illegal, but it is an offence to import or sell it.

Gambling

Gambling is illegal in Singapore with the following exceptions: charity draws, Toto and Singapore Sweep lotteries and on-course betting at the Bukit Turf Club.

Safety

Singapore has one of the lowest crime rates in the world. Pickpockets and bag-snatchers are rare, and women in Singapore generally feel safe to travel alone. Nevertheless, it makes sense to take the usual precautions. Keep a separate note of travellers' cheque and credit card numbers and don't leave valuables lying around.

INDEX